2.49

D0763216

For the Love of Soup

For the Love of Soup

Jeanelle Mitchell

whitecap

The information in this book is true and complete to the best of our knowledge. All recommendations are made without guarantee on the part of the author or Whitecap Books Ltd. The author and publisher disclaim any liability in connection with the use of this information. For additional information, please contact Whitecap Books Ltd., 351 Lynn Avenue, North Vancouver, British Columbia, Canada V7J 2C4.

Cover illustration: Mary Cassel
Interior illustrations: Jeanelle Mitchell
Production editor: Roger Michaud
Technical assistant: Dan Mitchell
Editing: Julie Mitchell
Proofing: Marial Shea
Interior design: Warren Clark
Cover design: Roberta Batchelor

Printed and bound in Canada

National Library of Canada Cataloguing in Publication Data

Mitchell, Jeanelle.
        For the love of soup

        Includes index.
        ISBN 1-55285-409-4
        ISBN 978-1-55285-409-9

        1. Soups. I. Title.
TX757.M572 2002   641.8'13   C2002-910985-X

The publisher acknowledges the financial support of the Government of Canada through the Book Publishing Industry Development Program and the province of British Columbia through the Book Publishing Tax Credit.

Dedication

This book is dedicated to my family and friends, who have believed in me and encouraged me to write this book, especially my nephew Yves who is severely handicapped.

Yves was disabled after a tragic auto accident some years ago and requires a great deal of support and therapy. He has been my inspiration for completing this book and I hope that my book proceeds will enable him to better help himself.

How Not To Eat Soup

Don't eat soup from the end of the spoon,
but from the side.
Don't gurgle, or draw in your breath,
or make other noises when eating soup.
Don't ask for a second service of soup.
Don't bite your bread. Break it off.
Don't break your bread into your soup.

Oliver Bell Bunce, 1884

Contents

True friends share food for thought
and thoughts of food!

Jenny Faw

Acknowledgments

This book would not have been possible without my best friend – my husband – Tim, and my two wonderful children Julie and Dan, who have given me love and encouragement.

I would also like to acknowledge those people who have offered ideas and lots of support: my patient brother Roger and his wife Suzanne, who launched me into the world of computer editing; Mary who painted the cover of *For the Love of Soup*; my art classmates who encouraged me to use my own illustrations for this book; Bev and Bob for their continuous support; Tracey for her valuable comments; and finally to family, friends and neighbours, who have savoured and sipped numerous bowls of soup along the way.

Many thanks to all these wonderful people who helped me achieve my long-time goal of writing a cookbook.

A Daughter's Note

By Julie

I consider myself extremely lucky to be the daughter of the author, the master soup chef! This extraordinary woman, my mom, has inspired me in many ways throughout my life. Her soups were a comfort to me as a little girl, and continue to be, even now that I'm 23.

I had the typical university experience in my first year, arriving home 30 pounds heavier! Due to digestion problems and lactose intolerance, I was forced to give up dairy products, meat and other rich foods. Thanks to Mom and her fabulous healthy cooking, all that weight was gone by the time I had to go back to school, just four months later. I have always benefited from Mom's healthy creativity in the kitchen. That summer home from university, I really needed a little special creativity to bring myself back to a healthy lifestyle. I discovered the true meaning of "we are what we eat." Proper diet really is preventive medicine.

In my second year at school, living on my own meant cooking my own meals. With help from Mom, I soon realized how little effort it takes to prepare delicious, nutritious soups. The soups were great for lunch and for leftover dinners when I had to rush to the library to study.

My healthy attitude towards food and my love for Mom's incredible soups has helped me make a lifestyle change. I really do feel better than ever! Try them for yourself, you'll see.

Cheers, and soup it up!

Introduction

My dream to travel the world was realized when I left my home town of Grand Falls, New Brunswick at the age of 18. My passion for good food began when I joined Canadian Airlines as a flight attendant. In my travels around the world, I became aware of many different cultures and the fascinating rituals that accompany the sharing of a meal with family and friends.

As I saw more of the world, I realized that food is a universal language. I found myself arriving home from trips excited about trying out a new recipe gathered on my travels. Not every new recipe came from a restaurant in an exotic locale though. The flight attendants with whom I worked were, and continue to be, a culturally diverse group and an important source of inspiration. While the passengers slept, we took turns taking crew rests, sharing stories of the great meals we had enjoyed and trading recipes.

Having recently retired, I have had the opportunity to achieve my long-time goal of writing a cookbook. I chose to write a soup cookbook because it is my very favourite food. The result of a good pot of soup is always the same: a nutritious and satisfying comfort food. It is easily prepared, easily digested, economical, and just plain good tasting.

In my own kitchen, I've taken a healthful approach to eating and discovered that all types of soups can be created in a low-fat, low-sodium form without compromising taste. All 100 recipes have been triple tested to guarantee maximum good taste.

Nothing is more nourishing to the mind, body and soul than being surrounded by good friends and family and sharing a delicious pot of homemade soup.

Some people like to paint pictures, or do gardening, or build a boat in the basement. Other people get a tremendous pleasure out of the kitchen, because cooking is just as creative and imaginative an activity as drawing, or wood carving or music.

Julia Child

Helpful Tips

Essentials for Creating Healthy and Delicious Soup

The process of making soup is nearly as satisfying as the end result and it's usually quite simple. Little needs to be done other than to chop ingredients and throw them into a saucepan. With some basic equipment, simple techniques and the freshest ingredients, you can't go wrong.

Equipment and Techniques

To start, you need a few simple kitchen tools, ones you probably already have:

- large saucepan with a lid
- sharp chef's and paring knives
- vegetable peeler
- scissors
- measuring cups and spoons
- large chopping board
- spoon with a long handle
- colander
- sieve
- soup ladle
- blender or food processor for puréeing

To **simmer** is to keep a liquid just below boiling point, with bubbles from the edges only. When simmering soup, remember to stir occasionally; this is essential so that your soup doesn't stick to the saucepan.

To **purée** soup you need a blender or food processor. A great tool to have is an immersion blender (hand blender) that you can use right in your saucepan when puréeing soups, saving time and mess. Blend just until the soup is smooth; too much blending will create a gummy texture. Be careful when blending hot ingredients. Start the blender on slow with the lid slightly open, then seal the lid and turn to high speed. Also, blend your soup in batches. No one likes scraping soup off the walls or ceiling. Trust me. When reheating puréed soup, use low heat and stir frequently so your soup does not stick to the bottom of your saucepan, or as an alternative, use a double boiler.

The **thickness and texture** of your finished product will vary depending on the size of your vegetables; therefore, if you finish making the soup and it's too thick, just add more liquid.

Soup is more flexible in terms of **portions** than many other foods. A range of servings is indicated in this book, as soup will provide more servings as a starter than as a main course.

Soup improves with age (up to a point, of course.) Most soups can be prepared days ahead of time, refrigerated and reheated upon demand. Sitting time brings out the rich, mellow taste of vegetables and herbs, with the ingredients and broth marinating and blending together to create even more flavour. When reheating soup, remember to simmer just until it is heated; you don't want to overcook it.

Soup will freeze well, but bear in mind that beans, rice and noodles may break down and soups with milk may have a slightly curdled appearance. Because of this, I prefer not to freeze my soups (stock excepted). Soup will last in the refrigerator for days—what a great way to have a meal ready for those busy days to come. I always find a family member or friend who is willing to share my pot of soup with me. If you wish to freeze your soups, be sure to leave a 1 inch/2.5 cm space at the top of the freezer container to allow for expansion of the soup as it freezes. Freeze the liquid in which vegetables were cooked for later use in stocks and soups. The liquid retains some of the nutrients lost from the vegetables and provides a flavourful substitute for plain water.

Ingredients

The best ingredients make the finest soup. Capture the essence and colours of the freshest vegetables by taking full advantage of each season's harvest as they become available. The end result will provide optimum nutritional benefits and taste.

Beans

Every cup of dry beans yields about $2\frac{1}{2}$ cups/625 ml of cooked beans. Dried beans should be stored in well-sealed jars in a dry place. They can last up to a year; however, it is best to use them within two or three months of buying. After that, the beans take more time to cook and taste less fresh. Sort and rinse beans, combine them in a large saucepan with 3 to 4 times their volume of water. Cover and soak for 8 hours or overnight. (During warm months, let beans soak in the refrigerator to prevent

For the Love of Soup

spoilage.) Discard the soaking water, add fresh water and bring the beans to a boil. Reduce heat, simmer and partially cover the beans until done. Most beans require 1 to 2 hours of cooking. The quick-soak method is to bring the water and beans to a boil, turn off heat and let stand covered for an hour or so.

I'd rather reach for canned beans when time is an issue than forego the pleasure of cooking with them. The essential difference between them and those you cook yourself is the sodium content. Drain and rinse canned beans well before using them to remove brine, which is where most of the salt is. (Health food stores carry canned beans packed without salt or sugar and these have the best texture.)

Bread (the ultimate soup companion)

Bread and soup go hand-in-hand. Avoid flimsy, wimpy white bread and choose freshly baked firm-textured breads. Crusty Italian and French breads complement most soups and soak up those flavourful broths. Focaccia (chewy Italian flatbread) is also wonderful with soup especially when serving soup as a main course. Cornbread is fabulous served with Cajun or Mexican soup.

Dairy Products and Alternatives

I love using low-fat buttermilk, milk, yogurt and sour cream in soup. Just because soup is creamy and rich tasting doesn't mean it is loaded with calories or is high in fat. I have used small amounts of low-fat dairy products with great success. Just remember that low-fat buttermilk, milk, yogurt and sour cream will curdle easily when heated, therefore the soup should not boil once added.

Buttermilk gets its silky creaminess from having been cultured with friendly bacteria in the same manner as yogurt or sour cream. Low-fat buttermilk has the same amount of fat as low-fat milk and gives you the same creamy taste and texture as cream without the extra calories.

For those of you who have diets restricted to dairy-free products, there are many alternatives available that are both very healthy and surprisingly delicious. Dairy products can be substituted with soymilk and dairy-free cheeses. For those soups that ask to be garnished with sour cream or yogurt, non-dairy sour cream and yogurt substitutes are available as well. These products are low in fat and taste very similar, if not better, than dairy products.

Garnishes

Complete your creation by adding a garnish as a finishing touch for enhanced presentation. Adding fresh herbs as a garnish creates an infusion of flavour and adds a contrast in colour and texture to your soup.

Whenever yogurt or sour cream is called for as a garnish, use a dollop on each serving. For a quick and impressive garnish, beat yogurt or sour cream with a wire whisk until smooth; ladle the soup into bowls and drizzle the yogurt or sour cream in a swirl pattern or buy some squirt bottles and fill them with yogurt or sour cream mixed with finely chopped herbs and create a swirl pattern on top of individual servings.

Chopped nuts and seeds add a crunch and are wonderful as a garnish for creamy soups. Roast nuts and seeds to intensify their flavour. Preheat oven to 350°F/180°C and roast for 6 to 8 minutes, tossing occasionally. Toast small seeds, such as sesame, in a dry pan and shake constantly until seeds are fragrant and lightly browned.

Croutons make a great topping for creamy, smooth soups, adding an interesting contrast in texture as well as flavour. Use day-old bread for easy slicing and remember that any kind of bread can be used. Pumpernickel, rye, whole wheat or crusty bread are all great choices. Cut the crust off the bread and brush the bread with olive oil or melted butter and slice into small cubes or make shapes with bread using cookie cutters and turn your soup presentation into a work of art. Spread on a baking sheet and toast in a 350°F/180°C oven. Bake, tossing occasionally for 10 to 12 minutes or until golden brown. Set aside and cool before using. To make herbed croutons, sprinkle a small amount of your favourite herb on croutons before baking. If stored croutons lose crispness, bake at 300°F/150°C for 3 to 5 minutes.

Herbs and Spices

Soups that are low in fat and sodium need a boost in flavour. Fresh herbs will help ensure that your soups have the most delicious taste possible. Their heavenly scent and flavour surpass those of the dried variety, so I urge you to choose fresh whenever you can.

- **To keep herbs longer** in the refrigerator, try treating them like a bouquet of flowers. Immerse the stems in a jar with 2 inches/5 cm of water. Cover loosely with a plastic bag, changing the water every 2 days. This way the herbs will stay fresh for several days.
- **To chop fresh herbs** rinse them under cold running water and dry thoroughly by gently patting with paper towels. If leaves are attached to woody stems, pull them off and then chop.

- **To freeze fresh herbs** mince the leaves by hand or use a food processor or blender, adding oil through the top while the motor is still running, until herbs look like paste. Place spoonfuls of the herb paste on a cookie sheet. Cover with plastic wrap or foil and freeze. When herbs are solid, place them in freezer bags or containers and store them in the freezer. For every cup of herbs use ¼ cup/50 ml of oil. Adding oil helps keep the colour of the herbs. Unless you are sure you want a given combination of herbs, do them separately. You can always combine a lump of parsley and a lump of basil later. Another method is to mince the leaves, spoon into ice cube trays, fill trays with water, and freeze. Thaw before using or toss a frozen cube into soup.
- **Adding fresh herbs at the end of cooking time** is my favourite way to add a last-minute burst of flavour to the soup.
- **Cilantro** is also called coriander or Chinese parsley. This herb has a pungent palate-awakening taste and is an excellent addition to many soups.
- **Do not substitute dry ginger for fresh;** gingerroot is completely different. Fresh ginger provides a delicate yet distinctive flavour. Freeze fresh ginger in a plastic bag. When needed, grate or cut the amount you need from the frozen root, then return the rest to the freezer.
- **Garlic** is a natural seasoning and will enhance the flavour of your soup. I believe in garlic's healing properties and love to use it as much as possible. If you see a green centre in a garlic clove, split the clove lengthwise and discard the green shoot, which is bitter. There is no substitute for fresh garlic.
- **Check your supply of dried herbs and spices** for freshness. Replace those that have been lurking at the back of the shelf for a year or two. They may have lost their flavour and spices may have become bitter. When using dried herbs, avoid powdered varieties of the herb, unless specified, and use dried leaves because these have a better flavour. When using dried herbs, crumble them with your fingers to release their flavours.
- **Remember that herbs decrease the need for salt.** Do a taste test at the end of cooking before adding salt to your soup. Often I omit it altogether, but when I find the need for salt, I use sea salt because it is natural. Sea salt is obtained from evaporated seawater and is high in vitamins and minerals and contains no chemical additives.
- **Freshly ground pepper** should always be added to the soup at the end of cooking to capture its full aromatic and spicy flavour.
- **Indian curry paste** is preferable to the dried variety. It has more depth of flavour and a richer colour.

Leeks

Be sure to wash leeks thoroughly, splitting down the middle and paying special care to the grit that hides where the green and white parts meet. To clean them, slit each one lengthwise, then swish it in a sink full of cold water. Rinse each leek under cool running water.

Meat, Poultry, Seafood and Alternatives

Meat, poultry and fish can be healthy sources of protein. Careful selection and preparation are important for reducing the amount of fat. Choose lean cuts of meat with little fat and before cooking trim any visible fat. To be sure you are getting lean ground meats ask your butcher to grind your choice cuts for you. Poultry and fish, without skin, are naturally low in fat.

If you are one of the many who, for reasons of health or lifestyle, have adopted a vegetarian diet, you have a number of delicious options. Meat can be substituted using textured vegetable protein granules. (TVP is made from soy flour.) Rehydrate it with an equal amount of water or stock and then use it to replace ground meat in your soup.

Tofu is also a good substitute. It absorbs flavour from other ingredients in the soup and is a great source of protein. Tofu should be stored in the refrigerator submerged in a container of cold water. The water should be changed daily.

There are a number of powders and broth cubes available that do not contain meat products. Health food stores usually carry a good selection.

Mushrooms

Mushrooms won't go slimy if you keep them stored in a paper bag in the vegetable crisper. When cleaning, wipe them with a damp paper towel or briefly rinse them under cool running water but never soak them. They'll absorb too much water, which will dilute their subtle flavour.

Oils

I like using olive oil because I love the taste. Olive oil has been around for a long time and the more we know about it, the more we learn about its great contribution to good health. Safflower oil has a delicate flavour and is also a healthy choice. Avoid using any oil stored in your cupboard for six months or longer, unless it hasn't been opened. A few recipes call for a small amount of butter, but feel free to use olive oil or safflower oil instead.

Peppers

When handling hot peppers, protect your skin from the heat. Be sure not to touch your face or eyes and immediately after handling hot peppers wash your hands well or wear rubber gloves.

Storing Vegetables

Vegetables like whole squash, turnip, onion and potatoes last longer when stored in a cool, dark place.

Tomatoes

To ripen tomatoes, place them in a paper bag and leave on the counter at room temperature. Never store tomatoes in the refrigerator; it numbs their delicate flavour. Remember that canned tomatoes tend to be high in sodium and if you are on a sodium-restricted diet, you may want to omit salt in your soup. (Again, health food stores carry no-sodium canned tomatoes.) If using whole canned tomatoes, the easiest way to cut them up is to dump them into a mixing bowl and snip them into smaller pieces using kitchen scissors.

*In order to create there must be a
dynamic force, and what force
is more potent than love?*

Igor Stravinsky

Blue Chip Stocks

Capture the Comfort and Nourishing Taste

All About Stocks

Homemade stock is flavourful, healthy and lets you control the fat and salt content in your soup. If you are not in the habit of making stock, you might think it's very time consuming but once you get started, you'll realize how easy it is.

If time is a factor or making stock just isn't high on your to-do list, you can buy fresh and frozen stock from specialty food stores or substitute a good quality canned, powdered, paste or cubed soup base. Be sure to read the nutritional information on the package to choose a brand that is as low in fat and sodium as possible. (Check your neighbourhood health food store for the best selection.)

Stock can be made up to 4 days ahead. Cover and refrigerate until thoroughly chilled and the fat has hardened on the surface, about 8 hours or overnight. Remove fat and discard. If you want to use a hot homemade stock immediately, set the clear liquid aside for 15 minutes to allow the fat to rise to the surface. Carefully remove the top layer of fat with a shallow metal spoon.

If the stock is to be kept longer, it is best to freeze it in small quantities. Be sure to leave a 1-inch/2.5-cm space at the top of the freezer container to allow for expansion of the stock as it freezes. Label the stock before freezing so you'll know what it is and when you made it. To use frozen stock, thaw it in the refrigerator or microwave.

For the Love of Soup

Chicken/Turkey Stock

Makes about 8 cups/2 L

Meaty chicken pieces provide a richly flavoured stock. For turkey stock, use a meaty turkey carcass or pieces of turkey instead of chicken. You might need additional water to cover the carcass.

3 lbs	chicken or turkey pieces, all skin and fat removed	1.5 kg
12 cups	cold water	3 L
2	onions, quartered	2
2	whole cloves garlic	2
2	carrots, scraped and cut into chunks	2
2	stalks celery, cut into chunks	2
4	sprigs fresh parsley	4
4	sprigs fresh thyme or 1 tsp/5 ml dried thyme	4
1	bay leaf	1
½ tsp	whole black peppercorns	2 ml
½ cup	white wine (optional)	125 ml

1. In a large stockpot, combine chicken or turkey pieces and water; bring to a boil. Skim off any froth that rises to the surface.
2. Add all other ingredients; reduce heat and simmer partially covered for 2 hours. Remove from heat and strain stock through a cheesecloth-lined sieve into a large bowl and gently press the solids with a spoon to extract the liquid. (Remove meat and store for later use.)
3. Allow stock to cool uncovered to room temperature. Cover and refrigerate until thoroughly chilled and the fat has hardened on the surface, about 8 hours. Remove fat and discard. Use within 4 days or freeze in containers for later use.

Beef Stock

Makes about 10 cups/2.5 L

Browning the ingredients will give a rich dark colour to the stock.

3 lbs	meaty beef bones or short beef ribs, cut into pieces	1.5 kg
2	onions, quartered	2
2	large carrots, cut into chunks	2
14 cups	cold water	3.5 L
2	whole cloves garlic	2
2	stalks celery, cut into chunks	2
4	sprigs fresh parsley	4
4	sprigs fresh thyme or 1 tsp/5 ml dried thyme	4
1	bay leaf	1
½ tsp	whole black peppercorns	2 ml
½ cup	red wine (optional)	125 ml

Preheat oven to 450 °F/220°C.

1. Spread beef pieces, onions and carrots on a roasting pan. Roast, stirring frequently, for 40 minutes or until well browned.
2. Place roasted beef pieces and vegetables in a large stockpot. Deglaze roasting pan with 1 cup/250 ml of water, scraping up any brown bits stuck to the pan, and add to stockpot.
3. Add remaining water and all other ingredients to stockpot. Bring just to a boil over medium heat. Skim off any froth that rises to the surface. Reduce heat and simmer for 3 hours, partially covered. Remove from heat and strain stock through a cheesecloth-lined sieve into a large bowl. (Remove beef and store for later use.) Gently press the solids with a spoon to extract the liquid.
4. Allow stock to cool uncovered to room temperature. Cover and refrigerate stock until thoroughly chilled and the fat has hardened on the surface, about 8 hours. Remove fat and discard. Use within 4 days or freeze in containers for later use.

↩ Tip: Veal shanks or oxtails also make a flavourful stock.

For the Love of Soup

Fish Stock

The best fish stock is made with the frames (including heads and tails).

3 lbs	chopped white-fleshed fish frames	1.5 kg
12 cups	cold water	3 L
2	onions, quartered	2
1	leek, white and light part only, sliced	1
2	stalks celery, cut into chunks	2
2	carrots, scraped and cut into chunks	2
2	sprigs fresh parsley	2
4	sprigs fresh thyme	4
	or 1 tsp/5 ml dried thyme	
½ tsp	whole black peppercorns	2 ml
1	bay leaf	1
½ cup	white wine (optional)	125 ml

1. In a large stockpot, combine all ingredients; bring to a boil. Skim off any froth that rises to the surface. Reduce heat and simmer partially covered for 1 hour. Remove from heat and strain stock through a cheesecloth-lined sieve into a large bowl. Gently press the solids with a spoon to extract the liquid.

2. Allow stock to cool uncovered to room temperature. Cover and refrigerate stock until thoroughly chilled and the fat has hardened on the surface, about 8 hours. Remove fat and discard. Use within 4 days or freeze in containers for later use.

Tip: Use fish bones from fish such as cod, haddock, snapper, sole or grouper. (Do not use oily fish such as salmon.)

Shellfish Stock

Makes about 5 cups / 1.25 L

The next time you peel shrimp, don't throw away the shells. Freeze them in bags or containers until you're ready to make a batch of stock. This flavourful stock is a wonderful base for fish soup.

1 tbsp	olive or safflower oil	15 ml
1 lb	shrimp shells, crushed	500 g
1	onion, quartered	1
2	cloves garlic, slightly crushed	2
1	large carrot, scraped and cut into chunks	1
1	stalk celery, cut into chunks	1
2	sprigs fresh parsley	2
1	bay leaf	1
2	sprigs fresh thyme	2
½ tsp	whole black peppercorns	2 ml
6 cups	water	1.5 L

1. In a large saucepan, heat oil over medium heat. Add shrimp shells and sauté, stirring frequently, until they turn pink. Add onion, garlic, carrot and celery; sauté for 5 minutes.
2. Add remaining ingredients and bring to a boil. Reduce heat and simmer for 30 minutes, partially covered. Remove from heat and strain the stock through a cheesecloth-lined sieve into a bowl.
3. Allow stock to cool uncovered to room temperature. Cover and refrigerate. Use within 4 days or freeze in containers for later use.

Tip: You can substitute shrimp shells with shells from crab or lobster (or a mix).

Vegetable Stock

Makes about 6 cups / 1.5 L

This easy-to-prepare stock is wonderful to have on hand.

1 tbsp	safflower or olive oil	15 ml
2	onions, quartered	2
1	large leek, white and light part only, sliced	1
2	stalks celery, cut into chunks	2
4	carrots, scraped and cut into chunks	4
2	parsnips, scraped and cut into chunks	2
1 cup	coarsely chopped mushrooms	250 ml
4	sprigs fresh parsley	4
4	sprigs fresh thyme	4
	or 1 tsp/5 ml dried thyme	
½ tsp	whole black peppercorns	2 ml
2	bay leaves	2
10 cups	cold water	2.5 L

1. In a large stockpot, heat oil over medium heat. Add onions, leek, celery, carrots, parsnips and mushrooms; sauté vegetables for 10 minutes, or until softened but not browned.

2. Add all other ingredients and bring to a boil. Reduce heat and simmer partially covered for 45 minutes. Remove from heat and strain through a cheesecloth-lined sieve into a large bowl and gently press the solids with a spoon to extract the liquid.

3. Allow stock to cool uncovered to room temperature. Cover and refrigerate. Use within 4 days or freeze in containers for later use.

Each day provides its own gifts.

Martial

Vegetable Soups

Capture the Essence of Fragrant Herbs

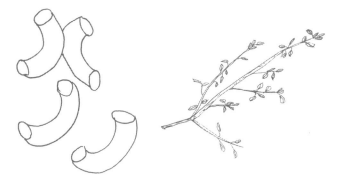

*Real generosity toward the future lies
in giving all to the present.*

Albert Camus

Asian Tofu & Noodle Soup

Serves 4 to 6

My daughter Julie, who developed a taste for Oriental flavours during her travels in Asia, inspired this soup.

2 oz	thin rice stick noodles (about 1 cup/250 ml)	60 g
2 tsp	sesame oil	10 ml
2	cloves garlic, minced	2
1 tsp	freshly grated gingerroot	5 ml
3 cups	low-sodium chicken or vegetable stock	750 ml
3 cups	water	750 ml
1 tbsp	low-sodium soy sauce	15 ml
8 oz	firm tofu, diced	250 g
2	carrots, scraped and thinly sliced	2
1 cup	small broccoli florets	250 ml
1 cup	snow peas	250 ml
2 cups	bok choy or napa cabbage	500 ml
2 cups	thinly sliced mushrooms	500 ml
1 cup	bean sprouts	250 ml
2	green onions, thinly sliced	2
	dash hot pepper sauce or to taste	

1. Place rice noodles in a medium bowl; pour boiling water over noodles to cover and let soak until noodles are tender, about 10 minutes. Drain and set aside.

2. In a large saucepan, heat oil over medium heat. Add garlic and gingerroot; sauté for 2 minutes. Add stock, water, and soy sauce; bring to a boil. Add tofu, carrots, broccoli, snow peas, cabbage, mushrooms and noodles; simmer uncovered for 4 minutes. Add bean sprouts and green onions and season with hot pepper sauce to taste.

Bean & Barley Soup

Serves 4

This hearty soup makes an ideal meal after an invigorating winter activity. The puréed beans lend a wonderful creamy texture.

½ cup	barley	125 ml
4 cups	water	1 L
2 cups	cooked or canned (drained and rinsed) red kidney beans	500 ml
1 tbsp	olive or safflower oil	15 ml
1	large onion, chopped	1
1	stalk celery, chopped	1
1	large carrot, scraped and chopped	1
2 cups	low-sodium chicken or vegetable stock	500 ml
2 cups	water	500 ml
2 tbsp	tomato paste	25 ml
2 tbsp	chopped fresh Italian parsley	25 ml
	sea salt and freshly ground pepper to taste	

1. Combine barley and water in a large saucepan; bring to a boil. Reduce heat, cover and simmer for 40 minutes, stirring occasionally.
2. Mash or purée half the beans and set aside.
3. In a large saucepan, heat oil over medium heat. Add onion and celery; sauté for 4 minutes. Add barley and cooking water, puréed and whole beans, carrot, stock, water and tomato paste; bring to a boil. Reduce heat, cover and simmer for 20 minutes, stirring occasionally. Add parsley and season with salt and pepper.

↪ Tip: If making ahead, keep in mind that the barley will continue to absorb liquid. Add a little extra stock or water when reheating.

Bowtie Pasta & Arugula in Broth

Serves 4

This light, easy-to-prepare soup is perfect as a first course. Arugula is a salad green with a peppery flavour and long bright green leaves.

2 tsp	olive oil	10 ml
2	cloves garlic, minced	2
4 cups	low-sodium chicken stock	1 L
1 cup	small bowtie pasta	250 ml
1cup	chopped fresh arugula	250 ml
1 tbsp	chopped Italian parsley	15 ml
	freshly ground pepper to taste	
Garnish:	freshly shaved Parmesan cheese (optional)	

1. In a large saucepan, heat oil over medium heat. Add garlic and sauté for 2 minutes. Add stock and bring to a boil.
2. Stir in pasta and cook for 10 minutes or until pasta is tender but firm.
3. Add Arugula and parsley; simmer for 3 minutes. Season with pepper and serve with Parmesan cheese, if desired.

Broccoli & Fennel Soup with Parmesan

Serves 4 to 6

The combination of broccoli and fennel gives a distinctive flavour to this soup. A sprinkle of Parmesan cheese at the end of cooking time adds a tantalizing savoury treat.

1 tbsp	olive or safflower oil	15 ml
1	onion, finely chopped	1
2	cloves garlic, minced	2
1	stalk celery, diced	1
1	medium fennel, diced, feathery green ends discarded	1
1	medium potato, peeled and diced	1
2 cups	small broccoli florets	500 ml
2 cups	low-sodium chicken or vegetable stock	500 ml
2 cups	water	500 ml
1 tsp	chopped fresh thyme or ¼ tsp/1 ml dried thyme	5 ml
1	bay leaf	1
	freshly ground pepper to taste	
3 tbsp	freshly grated Parmesan cheese	50 ml

1. In a large saucepan, heat oil over medium heat. Add onion, garlic and celery; sauté for 4 minutes. Add fennel, potato, broccoli, stock, water, thyme and bay leaf; bring to a boil. Reduce heat and simmer for 20 minutes, stirring occasionally. Remove bay leaf.
2. Season with pepper and stir in Parmesan cheese.

> ↩ Tip: For a creamy-textured broth, partially purée soup in the saucepan using an immersion blender or transfer a portion of the soup to a blender or food processor and blend until smooth. Return puréed portion back to the saucepan.

Chunky Lentil Soup

Serves 6 to 8

*This old-fashioned soup is nourishing and comforting. A
sprinkle of Parmesan cheese gives it an interesting flavour.*

1½ cups	brown or green lentils, picked over and rinsed	375 ml
2 tbsp	olive or safflower oil	25 ml
2	onions, diced	2
2	cloves garlic, minced	2
2	leeks, white and light parts only, cut in half lengthwise and thinly sliced	2
2	stalks celery, diced	2
4 cups	low-sodium chicken or vegetable stock	1 L
4 cups	water	1 L
2	medium carrots, scraped and diced	2
2	medium potatoes, peeled and diced	2
1 tbsp	chopped fresh thyme or 1 tsp/5 ml dried thyme	15 ml
2	bay leaves	2
3 tbsp	tomato paste	50 ml
1 tbsp	red wine vinegar	15 ml
	freshly ground pepper to taste	
Garnish:	Parmesan or mozzarella cheese (optional)	

1. In a large bowl, cover the lentils with boiling water, and let stand for 15 minutes. Drain and set aside.
2. In a large saucepan, heat oil over medium heat. Add onions, garlic, leeks and celery; sauté for 4 minutes.
3. Add stock, water, carrots, potatoes, lentils, thyme, bay leaves and tomato paste; bring to a boil. Reduce heat; cover and simmer for 40 to 50 minutes or until lentils are tender, stirring occasionally. Discard bay leaves. Add red wine vinegar and season with pepper. Serve with a sprinkle of Parmesan or mozzarella cheese, if desired.

Curried Cauliflower Soup

Serves 4 to 6

Partially puréeing this soup provides a smooth creamy base that combines wonderfully with the crunchy texture of the unpuréed ingredients.

1 tbsp	safflower oil	15 ml
1	onion, chopped	1
2	cloves garlic, minced	2
1	stalk celery, diced	1
2 tsp	mild curry paste	10 ml
½ tsp	ground cumin	2 ml
1 tsp	grated gingerroot	5 ml
¼ cup	long-grain white rice	50 ml
2 cups	low-sodium chicken or vegetable stock	500 ml
2 cups	water	500 ml
4 cups	chopped cauliflower	1 L
	sea salt and freshly ground pepper to taste	
Garnish:	low-fat yogurt or sour cream (optional)	
	snipped fresh chives, parsley or cilantro	

1. In a large saucepan, heat oil over medium heat. Add onion, garlic and celery; sauté for 4 minutes. Stir in curry, cumin, gingerroot and rice; cook for 2 minutes longer.
2. Add stock, water and cauliflower; bring to a boil. Reduce heat; cover and simmer for 20 minutes or until rice is tender, stirring occasionally. Remove from heat and cool slightly.
3. Partially purée soup in saucepan using an immersion blender or transfer half the soup to a blender or food processor and blend until smooth. Return puréed soup to saucepan. Simmer until heated and season with salt and pepper. Serve garnished with yogurt or sour cream, if desired, and snipped chives, parsley or cilantro.

Curried Red Lentil & Pasta Soup

Serves 4 to 6

Red lentils are tiny beans that require very little cooking time. This satisfying soup is ready in just minutes.

1 tbsp	safflower oil	15 ml
1	onion, finely chopped	1
2	cloves garlic, minced	2
1	stalk celery, diced	1
2	carrots, scraped and diced	2
1 tsp	mild curry paste	5 ml
2 cups	low-sodium chicken or vegetable stock	500 ml
2 cups	water	500 ml
½ cup	split red lentils	125 ml
1 cup	tomato juice	250 ml
2 tbsp	fresh lemon juice	25 ml
¾ cup	macaroni or other small-shape pasta	175 ml
	freshly ground pepper to taste	

1. In a large saucepan, heat oil over medium heat. Add onion, garlic, celery and carrots; sauté for 4 minutes. Stir in curry and cook for 1 minute longer.
2. Add stock, water, lentils, tomato juice and lemon juice; bring to a boil. Reduce heat, cover and simmer for 10 minutes.
3. Bring to a light boil, add pasta and cook for 10 minutes or until pasta is tender but firm, and season with pepper.

> ᐤ Tip: I use a small amount of curry so not to overpower other flavours in the soup, but if you like your soup spicier, feel free to add extra curry.

French Onion Soup

This recipe comes from my childhood friend Marcelle, who attended the Cordon Bleu School in Paris. Marcelle's version of this soup is lighter than the traditional recipe, but still magnifique!

3	medium onions	3
1 tbsp	unsalted butter	15 ml
2	cloves garlic, minced	2
1 tsp	sugar	5 ml
4 cups	low-sodium beef stock	1 L
½ cup	vermouth or dry white wine	125 ml
	freshly ground pepper to taste	
4	slices French bread	4
¾ cup	shredded low-fat Swiss cheese	175 ml

1. Cut onions in half lengthwise and cut crosswise into thin slices.
2. In a large saucepan, melt butter over medium heat. Add onions, garlic and sugar; cook covered for 15 minutes or until onions are tender and lightly coloured, stirring occasionally.
3. Add stock and vermouth or wine; bring to a boil. Reduce heat and simmer for 10 minutes. Season with pepper.
4. Meanwhile, toast bread under broiler until golden brown. Set aside.
5. Place four ovenproof soup bowls on a baking sheet; ladle soup into bowls. Top each bowl with a piece of toast and sprinkle cheese evenly on top. Broil for 2 or 3 minutes or until cheese is bubbly and golden. Serve immediately.

Curried Mushroom Soup

Serves 4

This soup has a wonderful rich colour and is full of flavour.

1 tbsp	safflower oil	15 ml
4	large shallots, finely chopped	4
6 cups	sliced brown or white mushrooms	1.5 L
1	carrot, scraped and diced	250 ml
2 tbsp	all-purpose flour	25 ml
1 tsp	mild curry paste	5 ml
2 cups	low-sodium chicken or vegetable stock	500 ml
2 cups	water	500 ml
½ cup	low-fat milk	125 ml
	sea salt and freshly ground pepper to taste	
Garnish:	chopped fresh chives or Italian parsley	

1. In a large saucepan, heat oil over medium heat. Add shallots, mushrooms and carrots; sauté for 4 minutes. Sprinkle flour over vegetables and stir in curry; cook for 2 minutes, stirring frequently.
2. Gradually stir in stock and water; bring to a boil. Reduce heat, cover and simmer for 15 minutes.
3. Stir in milk and simmer just until heated. Do not boil. Season with salt and pepper and serve garnished with chives or parsley.

> ↪ Tip: The shallot has a flavour that is similar to, but less pungent than, both garlic and onion.

Garlic & Egg Ribbon Soup

Serves 4

I first made this soup for a potluck luncheon given by my good friend Joanne. While we were sipping wine and talking about the good old days of flying, I completed the soup by adding the beaten eggs. The girls were impressed by how easy this soup was to prepare and of course, after lunch, they all took home a copy of the recipe.

1	whole garlic bulb	1
1	onion, coarsely chopped	1
1	stalk celery, coarsely chopped	1
2	sprigs fresh thyme	2
2	sprigs fresh parsley	2
4 cups	low-sodium chicken stock	1 L
2 cups	water	500 ml
2	eggs, lightly beaten	2
	dash hot pepper sauce or to taste	
Garnish:	chopped celery leaves	
	croutons (optional)	

1. Peel skin from garlic (see Tip). Slice garlic cloves and place in large saucepan.
2. Add onion, celery, thyme, parsley, stock and water; bring to a boil. Reduce heat, cover and simmer for 30 minutes. Strain through a fine sieve into a large bowl, pressing down on solids with a wooden spoon. (Soup can be made up to this point and refrigerated.)
3. Return soup to saucepan and bring to a simmer. Gradually add the beaten eggs in a slow stream, stirring constantly. Remove from heat, season with hot pepper sauce and serve immediately. Garnish with celery leaves and croutons, if desired.

⌐Tip: To quickly peel garlic cloves, trim off the ends and lightly crush the cloves with the flat blade of a large knife. The peel will come off easily.

Herbed Greens & Rice Soup

Serves 4 to 6

A wholesome, delicious winter soup your family will love.

2 tbsp	safflower or olive oil	25 ml
1	onion, chopped	1
3	green onions, chopped	3
1	leek, white and light part only, chopped	1
3	cloves garlic, minced	3
2	stalks celery, chopped	2
¼ cup	white rice	50 ml
4 cups	shredded green cabbage	1 L
2 cups	shredded Swiss chard, or kale	500 ml
4 cups	low-sodium chicken or vegetable stock	1 L
2 cups	water	500 ml
1	bay leaf	1
1 tsp	chopped fresh thyme	5 ml
	or ¼ tsp/1 ml dried thyme	
2 tsp	chopped fresh basil	10 ml
	or ½ tsp/2 ml dried basil	
3 tbsp	finely chopped fresh Italian parsley	50 ml
	sea salt and freshly ground pepper to taste	

1. In a large saucepan, heat oil over medium heat. Add onion, green onions, leek, garlic and celery; sauté for 4 minutes. Stir in rice and cook for 2 minutes longer.
2. Add cabbage, Swiss chard, stock, water, bay leaf, thyme and basil; bring to a boil. Reduce heat, cover and simmer for 20 minutes or until cabbage is tender. Remove bay leaf. Stir in parsley and season with salt and pepper.

> ᙧ Tip: For a creamy-textured broth, partially purée the soup in the saucepan using an immersion blender or transfer a portion of the soup to a blender or food processor and blend until smooth. Return puréed portion back into the saucepan.

Italian Zucchini & Rice Soup

Serves 4 to 6

This delicious soup is a snap to prepare. The Arborio or Italian short-grain rice has more starch than white rice, giving this soup a nice creamy consistency.

1 tbsp	olive oil	15 ml
1	onion, finely chopped	1
3	cloves garlic, minced	3
¼ cup	Italian short-grain rice	50 ml
2 cups	low-sodium chicken or vegetable stock	500 ml
2 cups	water	500 ml
3 tbsp	chopped fresh basil	50 ml
	or 1 tbsp/15 ml dried basil	
1 tbsp	chopped fresh oregano	15 ml
	or 1 tsp/5 ml dried oregano	
3	medium zucchini, diced	3
	(about 3 cups/750 ml)	
	sea salt and freshly ground pepper to taste	
Garnish:	freshly grated Parmesan cheese (optional)	

1. In a medium saucepan, heat oil over medium heat. Add onion and garlic; sauté for 4 minutes. Stir in rice and cook for 2 minutes longer.
2. Add stock, water, basil, oregano and zucchini and bring to a boil. Reduce heat, cover and simmer for 15 minutes.
3. Season with salt and pepper and serve with fresh Parmesan cheese, if desired.

> ↬ Tip: If this soup is made ahead, the rice will continue to absorb liquid. You may want to add extra stock or water when reheating. For a variation, try adding 2 cups/500 ml chopped fresh or canned tomatoes.

Porcini Mushroom Consommé

Serves 6 to 8

This elegant soup is a perfect starter. Dried mushrooms really intensify the flavour.

½ oz	dried porcini mushrooms	15 g
1 cup	boiling water	250 ml
1 tbsp	unsalted butter	15 ml
4	green onions, thinly sliced	4
3 cups	thinly sliced porcini mushroom caps	750 ml
1	carrot, scraped and finely diced	1
4 cups	low-sodium chicken or vegetable stock	1 L
2 cups	water	500 ml
2 tbsp	Madeira or port wine	25 ml
	sea salt and freshly ground pepper to taste	
Garnish:	snipped green onions, chives or parsley	

1. Rinse dried mushrooms with cold water to remove dirt granules. Place dried mushrooms in a bowl; pour 1 cup/250 ml of boiling water over the mushrooms and let stand for 15 minutes. Strain through a sieve lined with cheesecloth, reserving the liquid, and set aside.

2. In a large saucepan, melt butter over medium heat. Add green onions and fresh mushrooms; sauté for 5 minutes. Add carrot, stock, water, wine, reserved mushrooms and soaking liquid; bring to a boil. Reduce heat, cover and simmer for 10 minutes. Season with salt and pepper and serve garnished with green onions, chives or parsley.

> ↪ Tip: Wash fresh mushrooms quickly under cold running water and dry on paper towels. Mushrooms absorb water so it is best not to let them sit in water. Porcini mushrooms can be hard to find; you can substitute cremini mushrooms, sometimes referred to as brown mushrooms.

Mexican Tortilla Soup

Serves 6 to 8

Early in my career, an air traffic control strike grounded the flight crew in Acapulco for 6 days. Imagine how disappointed we were! On one of our many trips to local restaurants we discovered this zesty, satisfying soup.

1 tbsp	olive or safflower oil	15 ml
1	onion, chopped	1
1	sweet green pepper, diced	1
3	cloves garlic, minced	3
1	jalapeno pepper, seeded and finely chopped	1
1 tbsp	chili powder	15 ml
2 tbsp	chopped fresh oregano or 2 tsp/10 ml dried oregano	25 ml
1 tsp	ground cumin	5 ml
3 cups	low-sodium chicken or vegetable stock	750 ml
3 cups	water	750 ml
1	can (28 oz/796 ml) stewed tomatoes, chopped	1
1	medium zucchini, diced	1
1 cup	fresh or frozen corn kernels	250 ml
	sea salt and freshly ground pepper to taste	
6	small fresh flour tortillas, halved and cut in thin strips	6
Garnish:	grated Monterey Jack cheese or low-fat sour cream or yogurt (optional)	

1. In a large saucepan, heat oil over medium heat. Add onion, green pepper, garlic and jalapeno pepper; sauté for 4 minutes. Stir in chili powder, oregano and cumin; sauté for 2 minutes longer.
2. Add stock, water, tomatoes with juice, zucchini and corn; bring to a boil. Reduce heat and simmer for 20 minutes, stirring occasionally.
3. Season with salt and pepper, stir in tortilla strips and serve garnished with cheese, sour cream or yogurt, if desired.

> ✑ Tip: If making ahead of time, leave out the tortilla strips. When reheating, add tortilla strips just before serving.

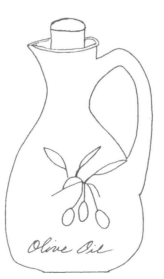

Olive Oil

Mexican Bean & Noodle Soup

Serves 4 to 6

This is one of the first recipes I ever scribbled down on my travels. I discovered it on a trip to Mexico, many years ago.

1 tbsp	olive or safflower oil	15 ml
1	onion, finely chopped	1
2	cloves garlic, minced	2
1	small, sweet green pepper, diced	1
1 tsp	chili powder	5 ml
2 tsp	chopped fresh oregano	10 ml
	or ½ tsp/2 ml dried oregano	
½ tsp	red pepper flakes or to taste	2 ml
3 cups	water	750 ml
1	can (19 oz/540 ml) tomato juice	1
1 cup	fresh or frozen corn kernels	250 ml
2 cups	cooked or canned (drained and rinsed) kidney beans	500 ml
¾ cup	broken spaghettini noodles	175 ml
2 tbsp	fresh lime juice	25 ml
Garnish:	chopped fresh cilantro or parsley	

1. In a large saucepan, heat oil over medium heat. Add onion, garlic and green pepper; sauté for 4 minutes. Stir in chili powder, oregano and red pepper flakes, cook for 2 minutes longer.
2. Add water, tomato juice, corn and beans; bring to a boil. Reduce heat, cover and simmer for 10 minutes.
3. Bring to a gentle boil, add noodles and cook 10 minutes or until noodles are tender. Stir in lime juice and serve garnished with chopped cilantro or parsley.

For the Love of Soup

Curried Pumpkin Soup with Mushrooms

Serves 4 to 6

The contrasting textures of smooth puréed pumpkin and slices of mushroom make this soup a little different from your ordinary pumpkin soup.

1 tbsp	unsalted butter	15 ml
1	onion, finely chopped	1
2	cloves garlic, minced	2
3 cups	sliced mushrooms	750 ml
2 tsp	mild curry paste	10 ml
2 cups	low-sodium chicken or vegetable stock	500 ml
1 cup	water	250 ml
2 tbsp	tomato paste	25 ml
1	can (19 oz/540 ml) pumpkin purée	1
	freshly ground pepper to taste	
Garnish:	low-fat sour cream or yogurt (optional)	

1. In a large saucepan, melt butter over medium heat. Add onion, garlic and mushrooms; sauté for 6 minutes. Stir in curry and cook for 2 minutes longer.
2. Add stock, water, tomato paste and pumpkin purée; bring to a boil. Reduce heat; cover and simmer for 10 minutes, stirring occasionally.
3. Season with pepper and serve with a swirl of sour cream or yogurt, if desired.

Minestrone

This hearty soup is a meal in itself. A rind from a piece of fresh Parmesan cheese adds texture and flavour to the soup. Whenever my nephew Yves comes for a visit, he requests this nutritious and comforting soup.

1 tbsp	olive oil	15 ml
1	onion, chopped	1
2	cloves garlic, minced	2
1	medium fennel bulb, diced, feathery green ends discarded, or 2 stalks celery, diced	1
3 cups	low-sodium chicken or vegetable stock	750 ml
3 cups	water	750 ml
2	carrots, scraped and sliced	2
2	medium potatoes, peeled and diced	2
1 cup	cut green beans (1-inch/2.5-cm pieces)	250 ml
1	can (28 oz/796 ml) plum tomatoes, chopped, or (2 lbs/1 kg) chopped fresh tomatoes	1
1	(2-inch/5-cm) piece of Parmesan rind (optional)	1
2 cups	cooked or canned (drained and rinsed) white or red kidney beans or chickpeas	500 ml
2	small zucchini, sliced	2
3 tbsp	chopped fresh Italian parsley	50 ml
½ cup	macaroni or other small-shape pasta freshly ground pepper to taste	125 ml
Garnish:	freshly shaved or grated Parmesan cheese (optional)	

1. In a large saucepan, heat oil over medium heat. Add onion, garlic and fennel or celery; sauté for 6 minutes.
2. Add stock, water, carrots, potatoes, green beans, tomatoes with juice and cheese rind if desired; bring to a boil. Reduce heat, cover and simmer for 25 minutes or until fennel is tender.
3. Add beans, zucchini and parsley; bring to a low boil. Stir in pasta, simmer for 10 minutes or until pasta is tender but firm, stirring occasionally. Discard cheese rind. Season with pepper and serve with Parmesan cheese, if desired.

> ↶ Tip: You may need to add some additional broth or water if you don't serve the soup as soon as it's finished cooking; as the soup stands the pasta continues to absorb liquid.

Portobello Mushroom
& Barley Soup

Serves 6

Mushrooms and barley are an excellent combination of flavours. The irresistible chewy texture of this soup will have you back for a second helping.

½ cup	barley	125 ml
4 cups	water	1 L
1 tbsp	unsalted butter	15 ml
1 tbsp	olive or safflower oil	15 ml
2	onions, chopped	2
4	cloves garlic, minced	4
1	stalk celery, diced	1
2	carrots, scraped and diced	2
6	medium portobello mushrooms, halved and sliced (about 4 cups/1 L)	6
4 cups	low-sodium chicken or vegetable stock	1 L
1 tbsp	fresh chopped basil or 1 tsp/5 ml dried basil	15 ml
1 tbsp	chopped fresh Italian parsley	15 ml
2 tbsp	fresh lemon juice	25 ml
	sea salt and freshly ground pepper to taste	

1. Combine barley and water in a large saucepan; bring to a boil. Reduce heat, cover and simmer for 40 minutes, stirring occasionally.
2. In a large saucepan, heat butter and oil over medium heat. Add onions, garlic, celery, carrots and mushrooms; sauté for 10 minutes.
3. Add barley and cooking water, stock, basil, parsley and lemon juice; bring to a boil. Reduce heat and simmer for 15 minutes. Season with salt and pepper.

> ↩ Tip: If making ahead of time, you'll find the barley will continue to absorb liquid. To thin the soup, add a little extra stock or water when reheating.

For the Love of Soup

Red Cabbage & Apple Soup

Serves 4 to 6

*This recipe is one of my more popular "special requests."
My daughter's friend Jen, who is both vegetarian and
lactose intolerant, loves this flavourful sweet-and-sour
soup. I often make it for her when she visits.*

1 tbsp	olive or safflower oil	15 ml
1	onion, finely chopped	1
2	cloves garlic, minced	2
2 tbsp	brown sugar	25 ml
2 tbsp	balsamic vinegar	25 ml
½ tsp	hot pepper flakes or to taste	2 ml
6 cups	shredded red cabbage	1.5 L
4 cups	low-sodium chicken or vegetable stock	1 L
2 cups	water	500 ml
1	can (19 oz/540 ml) tomatoes, chopped	1
2	apples, peeled, cored and diced	2
	sea salt and freshly ground pepper to taste	
Garnish:	low-fat sour cream or yogurt (optional)	

1. In a large saucepan, heat oil over medium heat. Add onion and garlic; sauté for 4 minutes. Stir in sugar, vinegar and hot pepper flakes and cook for 2 minutes. Add the cabbage and stir to combine.
2. Add stock, water and tomatoes with juice; bring to a boil. Reduce heat, cover and simmer for 20 to 30 minutes or until cabbage is tender, stirring occasionally. Add diced apples and simmer for 2 minutes longer. Season with salt and pepper and serve garnished with a dollop of sour cream or yogurt, if desired.

Stracciatella Soup

Serves 6 to 8

A flavourful classic Italian soup that is easy to prepare. In Italian, stracci means rags. When you add the eggs to the hot soup, they form a shape reminiscent of bits of rags.

6 cups	low-sodium chicken or vegetable stock	1.5 L
2 cups	water	500 ml
½ cup	orzo or other small soup noodle	125 ml
2 cups	chopped fresh spinach	500 ml
3 tbsp	chopped fresh basil	50 ml
	or 1 tbsp/15 ml dried basil	
2	eggs, lightly beaten	2
	sea salt and freshly ground pepper to taste	
Garnish:	freshly grated Parmesan cheese (optional)	

1. In a large saucepan, bring stock and water to a boil; add orzo and cook for 3 to 4 minutes or until noodles are tender but firm.
2. Stir in the spinach and basil; reduce heat and simmer for 2 minutes. Gradually add the beaten eggs in a slow stream, stirring constantly. Remove from heat and season with salt and pepper. Serve with Parmesan cheese, if desired.

Tomato & Rice Soup

Serves 4 to 6

This is my mother's recipe and the very first soup I ever made. My brother Roger, a part-time cook at best, swears this recipe has never failed him.

1 tbsp	olive or safflower oil	15 ml
1	medium onion, diced	1
2	stalks celery, diced	2
2	medium carrots, scraped and diced	2
¼ cup	long-grain rice	50 ml
2 cups	low-sodium chicken or vegetable stock	500 ml
2 cups	water	500 ml
1	can (19 oz/540 ml) diced tomatoes	1
2 tbsp	chopped fresh basil	25 ml
	or 2 tsp/10 ml dried basil	
	sea salt and freshly ground pepper to taste	
Garnish:	chopped fresh green onions or chives	

1. In a large saucepan, heat oil over medium heat. Add onion, celery and carrots; sauté for 4 minutes. Stir in rice and cook for 2 minutes.
2. Add stock, water, tomatoes with juice and basil; bring to a boil. Reduce heat, cover and simmer for 15 minutes or until rice is tender. Season with salt and pepper and serve garnished with green onions or chives.

Soupe au Pistou

Serves 6 to 8

I get rave reviews from my family and friends when I make this delicious soup. Pistou is the French version of Italy's Pesto.

1 tbsp	olive or safflower oil	15 ml
1	medium onion, chopped	1
2	cloves garlic, minced	2
1	stalk celery, chopped	1
3 cups	low-sodium chicken or vegetable stock	750 ml
3 cups	water	750 ml
1	carrot, scraped and sliced	1
1 cup	cut green beans (1-inch/2.5-cm pieces)	250 ml
1	large potato, peeled and diced	1
2 tbsp	chopped fresh basil	25 ml
1	can (28 oz/796 ml) plum tomatoes, chopped, or 2 lbs/1 kg fresh ripe tomatoes	1
½ cup	macaroni or other small-shape pasta	125 ml
1	zucchini, diced	1
	sea salt and freshly ground pepper to taste	
	Basil Pistou (see recipe)	

1. In a large saucepan, heat oil over medium heat. Add onion, garlic and celery; sauté for 4 minutes. Add stock, water, carrot, green beans, potato, basil and tomatoes with juice; bring to a boil.

2. Reduce heat, cover and simmer for 15 minutes. Return to a low boil; stir in pasta and zucchini, cook for 10 minutes or until pasta is firm but tender. Stir pistou into the soup and season with salt and pepper.

> ↩ Tip: If making soup to serve at a later time, stir in pistou just before serving.

Basil Pistou

1	clove garlic, minced	1
3 tbsp	chopped fresh basil	50 ml
1 tbsp	olive oil	15 ml
3 tbsp	freshly grated Parmesan cheese (optional)	50 ml

Combine the 4 ingredients in a small bowl and add to soup.

> ✑ Tip: If making pistou ahead of time, cover with a thin layer of oil before storing in the refrigerator to keep its bright colour. I make pistou in volume during the summer when fresh basil is bountiful and freeze it.
>
> Pistou keeps in the refrigerator for several days and freezes well. It is also delicious as a salad dressing. Just add lemon juice or vinegar and extra olive oil to taste and season with salt and pepper. Pistou is wonderful in pasta sauce, lightly spread on pizza dough and added to other soup recipes that contain basil.

Savoury Borscht

Serves 6 to 8

My neighbours, Bev and Bob, love this iron-rich soup. If you are like Bev and have garlic sensitivity, you can make this soup without garlic and not compromise the taste.

2 lbs	small fresh beets	1 kg
1 tbsp	olive or safflower oil	15 ml
1	onion, chopped	1
2	stalks celery, diced	2
2	cloves garlic, minced	2
1 tbsp	brown sugar	15 ml
2 tbsp	red wine vinegar	25 ml
2 cups	shredded green cabbage	500 ml
2	carrots, scraped and diced	2
1	potato, peeled and diced	1
2 cups	low-sodium beef or vegetable stock	500 ml
2 cups	water	500 ml
1	bay leaf	1
1 tbsp	chopped fresh thyme	15 ml
	or 1 tsp/5 ml dried thyme	
	sea salt and freshly ground pepper	
Garnish:	low-fat yogurt or sour cream (optional)	
	chopped fresh chives, parsley or dill	

1. Wash beets and trim, leaving a little of the ends attached. In a large saucepan, cover beets with 6 cups/1.5 L of water and bring to a boil. Reduce heat, cover and simmer for 30 minutes. Drain, reserving 3 cups/750 ml cooking liquid. Under cold running water, rub off the peel (peel will come off easily) remove the ends, dice beets and set aside.

2. In a large saucepan, heat oil over medium heat. Add onion, celery and garlic; sauté for 4 minutes. Stir in sugar, vinegar and cabbage; cook, stirring for 3 minutes longer.

3. Add beets and reserved cooking liquid, carrots, potato, stock, water, bay leaf and thyme; bring to a boil. Cover and simmer for 30 to 40 minutes or until the vegetable are tender, stirring occasionally. Remove bay leaf. Season with salt and pepper and serve garnished with yogurt or sour cream, if desired, and chives, parsley or dill.

Tomato Fennel Soup with Gremolata

Serves 4 to 6

Gremolata is a garnish made by combining parsley, garlic and lemon zest. The gremolata gives your taste buds a kick and adds a fresh, unique taste to the soup.

2 tbsp	olive or safflower oil	25 ml
1	medium fennel bulb, diced, feathery green ends discarded	1
1	onion, chopped	1
3	cloves garlic, minced	3
2 cups	low-sodium chicken or vegetable stock	500 ml
1 cup	water	250 ml
$\frac{1}{2}$ tsp	crushed fennel seeds	2 ml
1 tsp	sugar	5 ml
1	can (28 oz/796 ml) plum tomatoes, chopped	1
1	juice of 1 lemon	1
	sea salt and freshly ground pepper to taste	
Garnish:	Gremolata (see recipe)	

1. In a large saucepan, heat oil over medium heat. Add fennel, onion and garlic; sauté for 6 minutes.
2. Add stock, water, crushed fennel seeds, sugar and tomatoes with juice; bring to a boil. Reduce heat and simmer for 20 minutes, stirring occasionally. Add lemon juice and season with salt and pepper.
3. Serve garnished with a sprinkle of gremolata.

> ↩ Tip: This versatile soup can be served as is, or puréed. It is also delicious served chilled.

Gremolata

2 tbsp	chopped Italian parsley	25 ml
2	cloves garlic, minced	2
2 tsp	lemon zest	10 ml

Combine ingredients in a small bowl.

> ↩ Tip: Use only the thin, coloured outer layer of lemon rind. (The white pith is bitter).

Tortellini & Spinach in Broth

Serves 4

This soup is light enough to be served as a first course.

2 cups	low-sodium chicken or vegetable stock	500 ml
2 cups	water	500 ml
2	cloves garlic, minced	2
1 cup	chopped fresh or canned tomatoes	250 ml
1 tbsp	tomato paste	15 ml
8 oz	fresh cheese-filled tortellini	250 g
1 cup	torn spinach leaves	250 ml
3 tbsp	finely chopped fresh basil	50 ml
	freshly ground pepper to taste	
1 tsp	olive oil	5 ml
Garnish:	freshly shaved or grated Parmesan cheese (optional)	

1. In a large saucepan, add stock, water, garlic, tomatoes and tomato paste; bring to a boil. Add tortellini and cook for 4 to 6 minutes or until tortellini is tender but firm.
2. Stir in spinach and basil; simmer for 2 minutes. Season with pepper, drizzle with oil and serve garnished with Parmesan cheese, if desired.

Tuscan Bean Soup

Serves 6 to 8

This is a recipe I shared with my friend Pinky. She makes this soup regularly and gets rave reviews.

2 tbsp	olive oil	25 ml
1	large onion, finely chopped	1
3	cloves garlic, minced	3
2	stalks celery, diced	2
2	carrots, scraped and diced	2
2 cups	low-sodium chicken or vegetable stock	500 ml
2 cups	water	500 ml
1	can (28 oz/796 ml) plum tomatoes, chopped	1
4 cups	white kidney beans, cooked or canned (drained and rinsed)	1 L
3 tbsp	chopped fresh basil or 1 tbsp/15 ml dried basil	50 ml
½ cup	dry red wine sea salt and freshly ground pepper to taste	125 ml
Garnish:	freshly shaved or grated Parmesan cheese (optional)	

1. In a large saucepan heat oil over medium heat. Add onion, garlic, celery and carrots; sauté for 5 minutes. Add stock, water, tomatoes with juice, beans, basil and red wine; bring to a boil. Reduce heat, cover and simmer for 15 minutes, stirring occasionally.

2. Partially purée soup in saucepan using an immersion blender or transfer 2 cups/500 ml of the soup to a blender or food processor and blend until smooth. Return puréed soup back into the saucepan. Season with salt and pepper and simmer until heated. Serve with a sprinkle of Parmesan cheese, if desired.

Vegetarian Chili Soup

I first made this soup for my daughter Julie, who is a real vegetable enthusiast. It has become a favourite in her recipe collection.

2 tbsp	olive or safflower oil	25 ml
2	onions, chopped	2
2	cloves garlic, chopped	2
1	stalk celery, chopped	1
2	carrots, scraped and chopped	2
1	sweet green pepper, chopped	1
3 cups	diced eggplant	750 ml
2 cups	diced zucchini	500 ml
2 cups	sliced mushrooms	500 ml
1 tbsp	chili powder	15 ml
1 tsp	cumin powder	5 ml
3 cups	water	750 ml
½ cup	mild or medium salsa	125 ml
2 tbsp	chopped fresh basil	25 ml
	or 2 tsp/10 ml dried basil	
1	can (28 oz/796 ml) tomatoes, chopped	1
2 cups	kidney beans or chickpeas,	500 ml
	cooked or canned (drained and rinsed)	
	freshly ground pepper to taste	
Garnish:	crumbled low-fat feta cheese (optional)	

1. In a large saucepan, heat oil over medium heat. Add onions, garlic, celery, carrots, green pepper, eggplant, zucchini and mushrooms; sauté vegetables for 10 minutes. Stir in chili powder and cumin powder; sauté for 2 minutes longer.
2. Add water, salsa, basil, tomatoes with juice, and kidney beans or chickpeas; bring to a boil. Reduce heat, cover and simmer for 20 minutes, stirring occasionally. Season with pepper and serve garnished with feta cheese, if desired.

Wild Mushroom & Basmati Rice Soup

Serves 6

Wild mushrooms have an exotic, rich, earthy taste.
The sherry and Dijon mustard enhance the flavour
of this wonderful soup.

1 tbsp	unsalted butter	15 ml
2 cups	chopped shallots	500 ml
2	cloves garlic, minced	2
2	stalks celery, diced	2
6 cups	diced wild mushrooms, such as portobello, cremini or shiitake (stems removed)	1.5 L
1/3 cup	basmati rice	80 ml
2 tsp	Dijon mustard	10 ml
1/4 cup	dry sherry	50 ml
2 tsp	chopped fresh thyme or 1/2 tsp/2 ml dried thyme	10 ml
3 cups	low-sodium chicken or vegetable stock	750 ml
3 cups	water	750 ml
1 cup	low-fat milk	250 ml
2 tbsp	cornstarch	25 ml
	sea salt and freshly ground pepper to taste	
Garnish:	low-fat sour cream (optional)	

1. In a large saucepan, melt butter over medium heat. Add shallots, garlic, celery and mushrooms; sauté for 10 minutes. Stir in rice and cook for 2 minutes longer.
2. Add mustard, sherry, thyme, stock and water; bring to a boil. Reduce heat, cover and simmer for 20 minutes or until rice is very soft.
3. Combine milk and cornstarch in a jar with a tight fitting lid, shake until well blended and add to saucepan. Simmer until the soup starts to thicken slightly, about 5 minutes. Season with salt and pepper and serve garnished with a dollop of sour cream, if desired.

Wild Mushroom & Leek Soup with White Wine

Serves 4 to 6

The combination of exotic mushrooms and a splash of white wine makes this soup truly delightful.

1 tbsp	unsalted butter	15 ml
2	leeks, white and light parts only, thinly sliced	2
2	small carrots, scraped and thinly sliced	2
1	stalk celery, diced	1
2 cups	sliced wild mushrooms, such as portobello, cremini or shiitake (stems removed)	500 ml
2 tsp	chopped fresh thyme or ¹⁄₂ tsp/2 ml dried thyme	10 ml
¹⁄₂ tsp	paprika	2 ml
¹⁄₂ cup	dry white wine	125 ml
2 cups	low-sodium chicken or vegetable stock	500 ml
2 cups	water	500 ml
	sea salt and freshly ground pepper to taste	

1. In a large saucepan, melt butter over medium heat. Add leeks, carrots, celery and mushrooms; sauté for 5 minutes. Stir in thyme, paprika, and wine; cook for 3 minutes longer.
2. Add stock and water; bring to a boil. Reduce heat, cover and simmer for 15 minutes and season with salt and pepper.

Puréed Soups

Capture the Creamy Pleasures without the Guilt

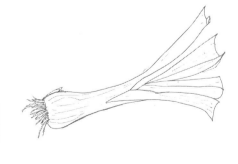

Our inventions mirror our secrect wishes.

Lawrence Durrell

Curried Zucchini & Leek Soup

Serves 4

*An easy-to-prepare soup that is delicious served either hot
or chilled. This soup will convert anyone who thinks
zucchini is bland. The curry and leeks really bring out the
flavour of this underappreciated vegetable.*

1 tbsp	safflower oil	15 ml
2	large leeks, white and light parts only, chopped	2
1 tsp	mild curry paste	5 ml
3 cups	water	750 ml
1	large baking potato, peeled and diced	1
2	large zucchini, chopped	2
Garnish:	low-fat yogurt or sour cream (optional)	

1. In a large saucepan, heat oil over medium heat. Add leeks; sauté for 4 minutes. Stir in curry and cook for 2 minutes longer.
2. Add water, potato and zucchini; bring to a boil. Reduce heat and simmer for 15 minutes or until the vegetables are tender. Remove from heat and cool slightly.
3. Purée soup in saucepan using an immersion blender or transfer in batches to a blender or food processor and blend until smooth. Return soup to saucepan and simmer until heated. Serve garnished with a swirl of yogurt or sour cream, if desired.

Creamy Cauliflower Soup

Serves 4 to 6

Everyone loves a velvety smooth cauliflower soup.
The combination of cauliflower and white rice gives
this soup its texture. The cheese is optional but I find
it gives the soup a little extra boost.

1 tbsp	unsalted butter	15 ml
2	leeks, white parts only, chopped	2
1	onion, chopped	1
2	stalks celery, chopped	2
2 cups	low-sodium chicken or vegetable stock	500 ml
4 cups	water	1 L
6 cups	chopped cauliflower	1.5 L
¼ cup	white rice	50 ml
1	bay leaf	1
	sea salt and freshly ground pepper to taste	
1 cup	grated low-fat cheddar cheese	250 ml
	or crumbled goat cheese (optional)	
Garnish:	chopped Italian parsley	

1. In a large saucepan, melt butter over medium heat. Add leeks, onion and celery; sauté for 4 minutes. Add stock, water, cauliflower, rice and bay leaf and bring to a boil. Reduce heat, cover and simmer for 20 minutes or until rice and vegetables are tender. Remove from heat, cool slightly and discard bay leaf.

2. Purée soup in saucepan using an immersion blender or transfer soup in batches to a blender or food processor and blend until smooth. Return to saucepan, season with salt and pepper and stir in cheese if desired. Simmer just until heated, do not boil, and serve garnished with parsley.

↪ Tip: If using cheddar cheese, remember to taste the soup before adding salt.

For the Love of Soup

Butternut Squash & Apple Soup

Serves 4 to 6

My brother-in-law Peter has an apple farm in Kimberley, Ontario. Every fall I use his fresh apples to make this soup. The apples add sweetness to the soup, complementing the buttery flavour and creamy texture of the squash.

1 tbsp	unsalted butter	15 ml
2	leeks white and light parts only, chopped	2
1	onion, chopped	1
2	cloves garlic, minced	2
1	large potato, peeled and diced	1
3 cups	diced, peeled butternut squash	750 ml
3	carrots, scraped and chopped	3
2	apples, peeled, cored and chopped	2
2 cups	low-sodium chicken or vegetable stock	500 ml
2 cups	water	500 ml
1 tbsp	fresh lemon juice	15 ml
1 cup	low-fat milk	250 ml
	sea salt and freshly ground pepper	
Garnish:	snipped fresh chives or parsley	

1. In a large saucepan, melt butter over medium heat. Add leeks, onion and garlic; sauté for 4 minutes.
2. Add potato, squash, carrots, apples, stock, water and lemon juice; bring to boil. Reduce heat, cover and simmer for 20 minutes or until vegetables are soft. Remove from heat and cool slightly.
3. Purée soup in the saucepan using an immersion blender or transfer in batches to a blender or food processor and blend until smooth.
4. Return soup to saucepan, stir in milk and season with salt and pepper; simmer until heated. Do not boil. Serve garnished with chives or parsley.

Creamy Chickpea Soup

This soup is quick and easy to prepare. The chickpeas provide an excellent source of protein and the little extra garlic adds a wonderful tangy taste.

1 tbsp	olive or safflower oil	15 ml
1	large leek, white and light part only, finely chopped	1
4	large cloves garlic, minced	4
1	large sweet red pepper, diced	1
2 cups	low-sodium chicken or vegetable stock	500 ml
2 cups	water	500 ml
2	cans (each 19 oz/540 ml) chickpeas, drained and rinsed	2
1 tsp	chopped fresh thyme or ¼ tsp/1 ml dried thyme	5 ml
1	bay leaf	1
2 tbsp	fresh lemon juice	25 ml
2 tbsp	chopped Italian parsley freshly ground pepper to taste	25 ml

1. In a large saucepan, heat oil over medium heat. Add leek, garlic, and red pepper; sauté for 4 minutes.
2. Add stock, water, chickpeas, thyme, bay leaf, lemon juice and parsley; bring to a boil. Reduce heat, cover and simmer for 15 minutes. Remove from heat, cool slightly and remove bay leaf.
3. Partially purée soup in the saucepan using an immersion blender or transfer a portion of the soup to a blender or food processor and blend until smooth. Pour the puréed soup back in the saucepan and simmer until heated. Season with pepper.

Creamy Leek & Fennel Soup with Parmesan

Serves 4 to 6

The subtle licorice flavour of the fennel is a delightful complement to the leeks. The Parmesan adds a final spark of flavour.

2 tbsp	safflower or olive oil	25 ml
2	leeks, white and light parts only, chopped	2
2	cloves garlic, minced	2
3	stalks celery, chopped	3
1	fennel bulb, chopped, feathery green ends discarded	1
1	large potato, peeled and chopped	1
3 cups	low-sodium chicken or vegetable stock	750 ml
3 cups	water	750 ml
1	juice of 1 lemon	1
	dash hot pepper sauce or to taste	
3 tbsp	finely chopped fresh Italian parsley	50 ml
3 tbsp	freshly grated Parmesan cheese	50 ml

1. In a large saucepan, heat oil over medium heat. Add leeks, garlic, celery and fennel; sauté for 6 minutes. Add potato, stock and water; bring to boil. Reduce heat, cover and simmer for 20 minutes; stir occasionally.

2. Purée soup in the saucepan using an immersion blender or transfer soup in batches to a blender or food processor and blend until smooth. Return to saucepan.

3. Stir in lemon juice, hot pepper sauce, parsley and Parmesan cheese and simmer just until heated. Do not boil. You may need to add additional stock or water for a thinner consistency.

Down-East Fiddlehead Soup

Serves 4 to 6

*Fiddleheads are the spring-fresh fronds of the ostrich fern,
plucked before they unravel. Wild fiddleheads grow in
abundance in New Brunswick and are a favourite in our
family. I have fond memories of picking fiddleheads with
my mother in the springtime. When they are available in
grocery stores I make this wonderful soup.*

12 cups	water	3 L
4 cups	fiddleheads	1 L
1 tbsp	olive or safflower oil	15 ml
2	leeks, white and light parts only, chopped	2
2	potatoes, peeled and diced	2
2 cups	low-sodium chicken or vegetable stock	500 ml
2 cups	water	500 ml
2 tbsp	fresh lemon juice	25 ml
	sea salt and freshly ground pepper to taste	
Garnish:	crumbled low-fat feta cheese	
	or low-fat sour cream (optional)	
	snipped fresh chives or Italian parsley	

1. Using a large saucepan, bring 12 cups/3 L of water to a boil; add fiddleheads and boil for 5 minutes. Drain and rinse fiddleheads in cold water and set aside.

2. In a large saucepan, heat oil over medium heat. Add leeks and sauté for 4 minutes. Add fiddleheads, potatoes, stock, water and lemon juice; bring to a boil. Reduce heat and simmer for 20 minutes, stirring occasionally. Remove from heat and cool slightly.

3. Purée soup in the saucepan using an immersion blender or transfer in batches to a blender or food processor and blend until smooth. Return soup to saucepan, simmer until heated and season with salt and pepper. Serve garnished with feta cheese or a dollop of sour cream and a sprinkle of snipped chives or parsley.

⤙Tip: Fresh fiddleheads are available in well-stocked grocery stores and are usually found in May and early June.

Puréed Soups

Golden Vegetable Soup

Serves 4 to 6

When my husband Tim and I were first married, I impressed my mother-in-law, "Mother Mitchell," on Thanksgiving with this golden root vegetable soup.

1 tbsp	olive or safflower oil	15 ml
1	onion, chopped	1
2	cloves garlic, chopped	2
1	stalk celery, chopped	1
1 tsp	grated fresh gingerroot	5 ml
3	medium carrots, scraped and chopped	3
2	medium parsnips, peeled and chopped	2
1	large potato, peeled and diced	1
2 cups	low-sodium chicken or vegetable stock	500 ml
2 cups	water	500 ml
½ cup	low-fat buttermilk	125 ml
	sea salt and freshly ground pepper to taste	
Garnish:	chopped fresh Italian parsley	

1. In large saucepan, heat oil over medium heat. Add onion, garlic and celery; sauté for 4 minutes. Stir in gingerroot and cook for 2 minutes longer.
2. Add carrots, parsnips, potato, stock and water; bring to a boil. Reduce heat, cover and simmer for 20 minutes or until vegetables are tender. Remove from heat and cool slightly.
3. Purée soup in saucepan using an immersion blender or transfer in batches to a blender or food processor and blend until smooth. Return soup to saucepan. Add buttermilk, season with salt and pepper and simmer until heated. Do not boil. Serve garnished with parsley.

> ✎ Tip: Low-fat buttermilk gives this soup the same creamy taste and texture as cream without the extra calories.

Herbed Carrot, Leek & Rice Soup

Serves 4 to 6

The green flecks of herbs give this partially puréed soup some colour and lots of flavour. The rice adds a thick, creamy texture without the calories!

2 tbsp	safflower or olive oil	25 ml
2	leeks, white and light parts only, chopped	2
1	onion, chopped	1
1	stalk celery, chopped	1
¼ cup	short-grain rice	50 ml
5	medium carrots, scraped and chopped (about 3 cups/750 ml)	5
3 cups	low-sodium chicken or vegetable stock	750 ml
3 cups	water	750 ml
1 tbsp	chopped fresh basil or 1 tsp/5 ml dried basil	15 ml
1 tsp	chopped fresh thyme or ¼ tsp/1 ml dried thyme	5 ml
4	sage leaves, chopped or ¼ tsp/1 ml dried sage sea salt and freshly ground pepper to taste	4
Garnish:	low-fat sour cream or yogurt (optional)	

1. In a large saucepan, heat oil over medium heat. Add leeks, onion, and celery; sauté for 4 minutes. Stir in rice and cook for 2 minutes longer.
2. Add carrots, stock, water, basil, thyme and sage; bring to a boil. Reduce heat, cover and simmer for 20 minutes or until rice is tender.
3. Partially purée soup in the saucepan using an immersion blender or transfer a portion of the soup to a blender or food processor and blend until smooth. Return puréed soup back to the saucepan and simmer until heated. Season with salt and pepper and serve garnished with sour cream or yogurt, if desired.

Ginger Orange Carrot Soup

Serves 6 to 8

Ginger and orange enhance this beta carotene-rich carrot soup. It is fresh, light and is also delicious served chilled.

1 tbsp	unsalted butter	15 ml
1 tbsp	safflower or olive oil	15 ml
1	large sweet onion	1
4 cups	scraped and chopped carrots	1 L
2 tsp	grated fresh gingerroot	10 ml
2 cups	low-sodium chicken or vegetable stock	500 ml
2 cups	water	500 ml
1 cup	orange juice	250 ml
	sea salt and freshly ground pepper to taste	
Garnish:	low-fat yogurt or sour cream (optional)	
	snipped fresh chives or Italian parsley	

1. In a large saucepan, melt butter with oil over medium heat. Add onion and carrots; sauté for 4 minutes. Stir in gingerroot and cook for 2 minutes longer.
2. Add stock, water and orange juice; bring to a boil. Reduce heat, cover and simmer 20 minutes or until carrots are tender. Remove from heat and cool slightly.
3. Purée soup in the saucepan using an immersion blender or transfer soup in batches to a blender or food processor and blend until smooth. Return to saucepan, season with salt and pepper and simmer until heated. Serve garnished with a dollop of yogurt or sour cream, if desired, and sprinkle with snipped chives or parsley.

For the Love of Soup

Creamy Broccoli Soup with Cheddar

Serves 4 to 6

My son Dan loves broccoli as long as it is topped with lots of cheese sauce. He enjoys adding a little extra cheddar when making this soup for his roommates.

1 tbsp	olive or safflower oil	15 ml
1	onion, chopped	1
2	cloves garlic, minced	2
1	stalk celery, chopped	1
1	carrot, scraped and chopped	1
2 cups	low-sodium chicken or vegetable stock	500 ml
1 cup	water	250 ml
3 cups	chopped broccoli	750 ml
1	large potato, peeled and cubed	1
1 cup	low-fat milk	250 ml
1 tbsp	Dijon mustard	15 ml
½ cup	grated, low-fat cheddar cheese (preferably old or medium)	125 ml
	sea salt and freshly ground pepper to taste	

1. In a large saucepan, heat oil over medium heat. Add onion, garlic, celery and carrot; sauté for 4 minutes. Add stock, water, broccoli and potato; bring to a boil. Reduce heat, cover and simmer for 15 minutes or until vegetables are tender. Remove from heat and cool slightly.

2. Purée soup in saucepan using an immersion blender, or transfer in batches to a blender or food processor and blend until smooth. Return soup to saucepan. Stir in milk, mustard and cheddar; simmer until cheese melts and soup is heated. Do not boil. Season with salt and pepper.

⤶ Tip: For a variation, replace broccoli with cauliflower.

Roasted Butternut Squash Soup

Serve 4 to 6

This soup has a sweet buttery flavour and creamy texture with few calories. My sister-in-law Suzanne describes this soup as "excellente."

1	butternut squash (2 lb/1 kg), cut in half and seeded	1
2 tbsp	olive or safflower oil	25 ml
2	leeks, white and light parts only, chopped	2
1	onion, chopped	1
1	large sweet potato, peeled and diced	1
2 cups	low-sodium chicken or vegetable stock	500 ml
2 cups	water	500 ml
1 tsp	chopped fresh thyme or ¼ tsp/1 ml dried thyme	5 ml
	sea salt and freshly ground pepper to taste	
Garnish:	low-fat sour cream or yogurt (optional) sunflower seeds	

Preheat oven to 350°F/180°C.

1. Cover baking sheet with parchment paper or foil. Brush squash with 1 tbsp/15 ml of oil and place cut side down on baking sheet. Roast for 40 minutes. When cool enough to handle, scoop out flesh into a bowl and discard skins. Set aside.

2. In a large saucepan, heat remaining oil over medium heat. Add leeks and onion; sauté for 4 minutes. Add sweet potato, stock, water and thyme; bring to a boil. Reduce heat, cover and simmer for 15 minutes, stirring occasionally. Add roasted squash and continue to simmer until vegetables are tender. Remove from heat and let cool slightly.

For the Love of Soup

3. Purée soup in saucepan using an immersion blender or transfer in batches to a blender or food processor and blend until smooth. Return to saucepan, simmer until heated and season with salt and pepper. (You may need to add additional stock or water for a thinner consistency.) Serve garnished with a dollop of sour cream or yogurt, if desired, and sunflower seeds.

⟲ Tip: My daughter Julie adds 1 cup/250 ml of soymilk after the soup has been puréed.

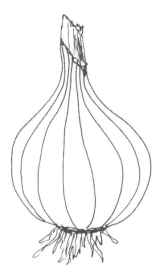

Roasted Celery Root Soup

Serves 6 to 8

Celery root, also known as celeriac, has a unique flavour. It is a knobby looking vegetable that resembles a wrinkly turnip. Don't be put off by its appearance; it is a delicious vegetable and roasting brings out its sweetness.

4 cups	peeled and cubed celery root	1 L
2 tbsp	olive or safflower oil	25 ml
1	onion, chopped	1
2	cloves garlic, chopped	2
2	stalks celery, chopped	2
1	leek, white and light part only, chopped	1
1	baking potato, peeled and chopped	1
2 cups	low-sodium chicken or vegetable stock	500 ml
2 cups	water	500 ml
1 tsp	chopped fresh thyme, or ¼ tsp/1 ml dried thyme	5 ml
1 tbsp	chopped fresh tarragon or 1 tsp/5 ml dried tarragon	15 ml
3 tbsp	chopped fresh Italian parsley	50 ml
½ cup	low-fat milk (optional) sea salt and freshly ground pepper	125 ml

Preheat oven to 350°F/180°C.

1. Toss celery root with 1 tbsp/15 ml of oil and place on a baking sheet; roast for 30 minutes, stirring occasionally.
2. In a large saucepan, heat remaining oil over medium heat. Add onion, garlic, celery and leek; sauté for 4 minutes.
3. Add potato, stock, water, thyme, tarragon and parsley; bring to a boil. Reduce heat, cover and simmer for 20 minutes. Add celery root and cook for 10 minutes or until vegetables are tender. Remove from heat and cool slightly.

4. Purée soup in the saucepan using an immersion blender or transfer soup in batches to a blender or food processor and blend until smooth. Return to saucepan and add milk, if desired. Season with salt and pepper and simmer until heated. (You may want to add extra milk or water for a thinner consistency.)

> ↬ Tip: The smaller roots are better; large ones tend to be hollow and woody. Because the flesh will darken quickly when exposed to air, peel celery root just before roasting.

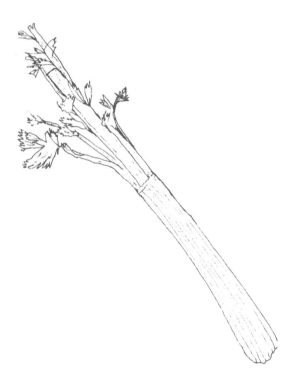

Roasted Asparagus Soup with Goat Cheese

Serves 6 to 8

Roasting concentrates the flavour of the asparagus and lightly caramelizes its peel, making the most of its delicate taste.

3 lbs	asparagus	1.5 kg
1 tsp	olive or safflower oil	5 ml
1 tbsp	unsalted butter	15 ml
2	leeks, white and light parts only, finely chopped	2
1	onion, chopped	1
1	stalk celery, chopped	1
3 cups	low-sodium chicken or vegetable stock	750 ml
3 cups	water	750 ml
	sea salt and freshly ground pepper to taste	
Garnish:	crumbled goat cheese (optional)	

Preheat oven to 400°F/200°C.

1. Trim off woody ends of asparagus by bending each stalk until it breaks. (It will snap off where it begins to toughen.) Wash asparagus well to remove any grit.
2. Spread asparagus on a baking sheet and drizzle with oil. Bake for 15 to 20 minutes turning occasionally, until tender. Remove from oven. Cut off tips and reserve for garnish. Chop remaining asparagus.
3. In a large saucepan, melt butter over medium heat. Add leeks, onion and celery; sauté for 6 minutes. Add stock and water; bring to a boil. Reduce heat, cover and simmer for 10 minutes. Add chopped asparagus to soup, remove from heat and cool slightly.
4. Purée soup in the saucepan using an immersion blender or transfer in batches to a blender or food processor and blend until smooth. Return soup to saucepan and add asparagus tips. Simmer until heated and season with salt and pepper. Garnish with crumbled goat cheese, if desired.

For the Love of Soup

Roasted Eggplant Soup with Goat Cheese

Serves 4 to 6

Roasting captures the essence of the vegetables and gives this soup its fabulous flavour.

1	large eggplant, halved lengthwise	1
1	onion, quartered	1
2	large carrots, scraped and cut into chunks	2
4	cloves garlic, peeled	4
1 tbsp	olive oil	15 ml
2 cups	low-sodium chicken or vegetable stock	500 ml
2 cups	water	500 ml
2 tbsp	tomato paste	25 ml
2 tsp	chopped fresh thyme	10 ml
	or $^1/_2$ tsp/2 ml dried thyme	
	sea salt and freshly ground pepper to taste	
Garnish:	low-fat crumbled goat cheese (optional)	

Preheat oven to 375°F/190°C.

1. Place eggplant, onion, carrots and garlic on baking sheet and brush vegetables with oil; roast for 40 minutes. When cool enough to handle, scrape out flesh from eggplant, discard skin, and place into large saucepan along with other roasted vegetables, stock, water, tomato paste and thyme; bring to a boil. Reduce heat, cover and simmer for 20 minutes or until vegetables are tender. Remove from heat and cool slightly.

2. Purée soup in the saucepan using an immersion blender or transfer in batches to a blender or food processor and blend until smooth. Return to saucepan and simmer until heated. Season with salt and pepper and serve garnished with goat cheese, if desired.

Roasted Parsnip Soup

Serves 4 to 6

This soup is sweet, creamy and delightful.

1½ lbs	parsnips, peeled	750 g
1 tbsp	olive or safflower oil	15 ml
¼ cup	water	50 ml
1	small onion, finely chopped	1
2	apples, peeled, cored and chopped	2
4 cups	low-sodium vegetable stock	1 L
¼ tsp	ground cinnamon	1 ml
2 tsp	chopped fresh thyme or 1 tsp/5 ml dried thyme	10 ml
1 cup	low-fat milk	250 ml
	sea salt and freshly ground pepper to taste	

Preheat oven to 350°F/180°C.

1. Cut parsnips crosswise into 2-inch/5-cm pieces, thick end pieces cut lengthwise in 1-inch/2.5-cm slices. Layer parsnips in roasting pan, drizzle with oil and toss to coat. Roast for 20 minutes, pour water on top, toss and cover with foil; continue to roast for 20 minutes longer. Remove from oven and set aside.
2. Meanwhile in a large saucepan add onion, apples, stock, cinnamon and thyme; bring to a boil. Reduce heat, cover and simmer for 10 minutes.
3. Add parsnips and continue to simmer for 10 minutes longer. Remove from heat and let cool slightly.
4. Purée soup in the saucepan using an immersion blender, or transfer in batches to a blender or food processor and blend until smooth. Return to saucepan and add milk; simmer until heated. Do not boil. Season with salt and pepper.

> ⋄ Tip: You can substitute low-fat buttermilk for milk. The soup will be richer, yet without extra calories.

Roasted Red Pepper Soup

Serves 4 to 6

Roasting red peppers takes a little extra time but it is well worth the effort. It's the roasted peppers that give this soup its zesty, full-bodied flavour.

4	large sweet red peppers	4
1 tbsp	olive or safflower oil	15 ml
2	leeks, white and light parts only, chopped	2
1	medium onion, chopped	1
2	cloves garlic, minced	2
2	large ripe tomatoes, chopped	2
2 tbsp	tomato paste	25 ml
2 cups	low-sodium chicken or vegetable stock	500 ml
2 cups	water	500 ml
1 tbsp	balsamic vinegar	15 ml
3 tbsp	chopped fresh basil	50 ml
	or 1 tbsp/15 ml dried basil	
	sea salt and freshly ground pepper to taste	
Garnish:	chopped fresh chives or basil	

Preheat broiler or barbecue grill.

1. Roast peppers under broiler or on grill until skins are charred black. Place in a paper bag; close and leave peppers in bag for 15 minutes. Peel, stem and remove seeds from peppers. Chop peppers coarsely and set aside.
2. In a large saucepan, heat oil over medium heat. Add leeks, onion and garlic; sauté for 4 minutes. Add roasted chopped peppers, tomatoes, tomato paste, stock, water, vinegar and basil; bring to a boil. Reduce heat and simmer for 15 minutes or until vegetables are tender. Remove from heat and cool slightly.
3. Purée soup in saucepan using an immersion blender or transfer soup in batches to a blender or food processor and blend until smooth. Return soup to saucepan and season with salt and pepper. Simmer until heated and serve garnished with fresh chives or basil.

Roasted Tomato Soup
with Lemon Grass

Serves 4 to 6

The fresh zing of lemon grass adds a refreshing taste to this soup. Delicious hot or cold.

3	stalks fresh lemon grass	3
1 tbsp	olive or safflower oil	15 ml
6	cloves garlic, peeled	6
3 lbs	fresh ripe tomatoes, halved	1.5 kg
2	onions, each cut into 8 wedges	2
2 tsp	chopped fresh thyme	10 ml
	or ½ tsp/2 ml dried thyme	
1 tsp	sugar	5 ml
2 cups	low-sodium chicken or vegetable stock	500 ml
	sea salt and freshly ground pepper to taste	
Garnish:	snipped fresh chives or Italian parsley	

Preheat oven 375°F/190°C.

1. Discard 1 or 2 outer leaves off each stalk of lemon grass and trim root ends. Finely chop the lower half of stalks, discarding the remaining pieces, and set aside.

2. Brush 1 tsp/5 ml of olive oil on a large shallow roasting pan. Place garlic, tomatoes (cut side up) and onion wedges in pan; brush vegetables with remaining oil. Sprinkle with lemon grass, thyme and sugar. Roast uncovered for 40 to 50 minutes or until onions are soft, tossing occasionally. Remove from oven, transfer to a large saucepan and stir in stock.

3. Purée soup in saucepan using an immersion blender or transfer to a blender or food processor in batches, if necessary, and purée until smooth. Strain soup through a sieve and return to the saucepan. Add water to thin soup to desired consistency. Season with salt and pepper to taste and simmer until heated. Serve garnished with chives or parsley.

For the Love of Soup

Roasted Vegetable Soup

As the fragrance of roasting vegetables fills the air, you will look forward to enjoying this delightful soup.

1	whole head garlic	1
1	onion, cut into 8 wedges	1
2	medium carrots, scraped and cut into chunks	2
1	fennel bulb, trimmed and cut into chunks	1
1	large baking potato peeled and cut into chunks	1
2 tbsp	olive or safflower oil	25 ml
2 tsp	chopped fresh rosemary or ½ tsp/2 ml dried rosemary	10 ml
2 tsp	chopped fresh thyme or ½ tsp/2 ml dried thyme	10 ml
4 cups	low-sodium chicken or vegetable stock	1 L
2 cups	water	500 ml
1 cup	low-fat milk	250 ml
	sea salt and freshly ground pepper to taste	
Garnish:	chopped fresh Italian parsley or chives	

Preheat oven to 400°F/200°C.

1. Cut ½ inch/1 cm off the top of garlic. Place garlic and vegetables on a baking sheet that is covered in parchment paper or foil. Drizzle oil over vegetables and sprinkle with rosemary and thyme. Roast in oven for 40 minutes, tossing occasionally. Transfer vegetables to a large saucepan. Squeeze garlic out of peel into the pan.

2. Stir in stock and water; bring to a boil. Simmer for 15 minutes or until vegetables are very tender, stirring occasionally. Remove from heat and cool slightly.

3. Purée soup in the saucepan using an immersion blender or transfer soup in batches to a blender or food processor and blend until smooth. Return soup to saucepan, stir in milk and simmer until heated. Do not boil. Season with salt and pepper and serve garnished with parsley or chives.

Roasted Sweet Potato Soup with Ginger Crisp

Serves 4 to 6

Roasting sweet potatoes with a small amount of brown sugar creates a sweet and distinctive taste.

1½ lbs	sweet potatoes, peeled and cubed (about 4 cups/1 L)	750 g
1 tbsp	olive or safflower oil	15 ml
1 tbsp	brown sugar	15 ml
1 tbsp	unsalted butter	15 ml
2	medium leeks, white and light parts only, finely chopped	2
2	stalks celery, finely chopped	2
1 tsp	freshly grated gingerroot	5 ml
2 cups	low-sodium chicken or vegetable stock	500 ml
2 cups	water	500 ml
1 cup	orange juice	250 ml
	sea salt and freshly ground pepper to taste	
Garnish:	Ginger Crisp (see recipe)	
	fresh chives, cut into 2-inch/5-cm lengths or fresh cilantro leaves	

Preheat oven to 400°F/200°C.

1. In a bowl, toss sweet potato cubes with olive oil and brown sugar. Spread on a large baking sheet and roast on top rack of preheated oven for 30 minutes or until lightly browned, stirring occasionally.
2. In a large saucepan, melt butter over medium heat. Add leeks and celery; sauté for 4 minutes. Add gingerroot and cook for 1 minute longer.

3. Add stock, water, orange juice and roasted sweet potatoes; bring to a boil. Reduce heat, cover and simmer for 20 minutes. Remove from heat and cool slightly.

4. Purée soup in the saucepan using an immersion blender or transfer in batches to a blender or food processor and blend until smooth. Return soup to saucepan. Season with salt and pepper and simmer until heated. Ladle soup into bowls and serve garnished with ginger crisp and chives or cilantro.

↜ Tip: Instead of ginger crisp, substitute fresh grated gingerroot. Stir into the soup just before serving.

Ginger Crisp

2 tbsp	safflower oil	25 ml
3 tbsp	peeled and thinly sliced gingerroot, cut into slivers	50 ml

Fry ginger strips in oil until pale golden and crisp. Drain on paper towel.

Roasted Tomato Garlic Soup

Serves 4 to 6

*Roasting vegetables adds an interesting smoky taste to
soups. Delicious served chilled on a hot summer day.*

3 lbs	ripe plum tomatoes	1.5 kg
1	whole head garlic	1
2	onions, each cut in eight wedges	2
2	carrots, scraped and cut in chunks	2
1 tbsp	olive or safflower oil	15 ml
2 cups	low-sodium chicken or vegetable stock	500 ml
1 cup	water	250 ml
¼ cup	chopped fresh basil	50 ml
	sea salt and freshly ground pepper to taste	

Preheat oven to 375°F/190°C.

1. Trim stem end of tomatoes and cut in half lengthwise. Place tomatoes, cut side up, on a large foil-lined baking sheet. Cut ½ inch/1.25 cm off the top of garlic; place garlic, onions and carrots on baking sheet with the tomatoes. Lightly brush vegetables with oil.
2. Roast for 40 to 50 minutes or until vegetables are soft. When cool enough to handle, remove garlic pulp by gently squeezing garlic cloves and remove skin from tomatoes.
3. Place roasted garlic, tomatoes, onions and carrots in a large saucepan. Add stock, water and basil; bring to a boil. Reduce heat and simmer for 10 minutes. Remove from heat and let cool slightly.
4. Purée soup in the saucepan using an immersion blender or transfer in batches to a blender or food processor and blend until smooth. Return soup to saucepan; season with salt and pepper and simmer until heated.

Papa Joe's Tomato Soup

My father-in-law "Papa Joe" loves tomato soup. I used this soup recipe to lure him away from those high-sodium canned soups. Delicious hot or cold.

1 tbsp	olive or safflower oil	15 ml
2	onions, chopped	2
2	cloves garlic, minced	2
1	can (28 oz/796 ml) tomatoes	1
2 tbsp	chopped fresh basil	25 ml
	or 2 tsp/10 ml dried basil	
1 cup	low-sodium chicken or vegetable stock	250 ml
1 cup	water	250 ml
2 tsp	sugar	10 ml
1 tbsp	balsamic vinegar	15 ml
	dash hot pepper or to taste	
	sea salt and freshly ground pepper	

1. In a large saucepan, heat oil over medium heat. Add onion and garlic; sauté for 4 minutes. Add tomatoes with juice, basil, stock, water, sugar, vinegar and hot pepper sauce; bring to a boil. Reduce heat and simmer for 30 minutes. Remove from heat and cool slightly.
2. Purée soup in saucepan using an immersion blender or transfer in batches to a blender or food processor and blend until smooth. Return to saucepan, season with salt and pepper and simmer until heated.

Root Vegetable Soup with Tarragon & Dijon

Serves 6 to 8

Tarragon has a distinctive taste and enhances the flavour of the root vegetables in this soup. The Dijon gives it a little extra kick!

1 tbsp	olive or safflower oil	15 ml
3	leeks, white and light parts only, chopped	3
1	onion, chopped	1
2	cloves garlic, minced	2
2	stalks celery, chopped	2
4 cups	low-sodium chicken or vegetable stock	1 L
4 cups	water	1 L
2	carrots, scraped and chopped	2
2	parsnips, peeled and chopped	2
2	potatoes, peeled and chopped	2
2 tbsp	chopped fresh tarragon	25 ml
	or 2 tsp/10 ml dried tarragon	
1 tbsp	Dijon mustard	15 ml
	sea salt and freshly ground pepper	
Garnish:	low-fat sour cream or yogurt (optional)	
	snipped fresh chives or Italian parsley	

1. In a large saucepan, heat oil over medium heat. Add leeks, onion, garlic and celery; sauté for 4 minutes. Add stock, water, carrots, parsnips, potatoes, tarragon and Dijon; bring to a boil. Reduce heat, cover and simmer for 25 minutes or until vegetables are tender. Remove from heat and cool slightly.

2. Purée soup in the saucepan using an immersion blender or transfer soup in batches to a blender or food processor and blend until smooth. Return to saucepan, season with salt and pepper and simmer until heated.

3. Serve garnished with a dollop of sour cream or yogurt, if desired, and snipped fresh chives or parsley.

For the Love of Soup

Szechuan Carrot Soup

Serves 4 to 6

This is an interesting twist on an old favourite. The peanut sauce gives this soup a unique and delightful flavour.

1 tbsp	olive or safflower oil	15 ml
1	onion, chopped	1
1	stalk celery, chopped	1
2	cloves garlic, minced	2
2 tsp	grated fresh gingerroot	10 ml
4 cups	scraped, chopped carrots	1 L
2 cups	low-sodium chicken or vegetable stock	500 ml
1 cup	water	250 ml
⅓ cup	Szechuan peanut sauce	80 ml
1 cup	low-fat milk	250 ml
Garnish:	chopped fresh cilantro or Italian parsley	

1. In a large saucepan, heat oil over medium heat. Add onion, celery and garlic; sauté for 4 minutes. Stir in gingerroot and cook for 2 minutes longer.
2. Add carrots, stock and water; bring to a boil. Reduce heat, cover and simmer for 20 minutes. Remove from heat and cool slightly.
3. Purée soup in the saucepan using an immersion blender or transfer in batches to a blender or food processor and blend until smooth. Return to saucepan, add peanut sauce and milk and simmer until heated. Do not boil. Serve garnished with cilantro or parsley.

↩ Tip: This soup is also delicious served chilled.

Spring Vegetable Soup with Buttermilk

Serves 6

Buttermilk gives this soup a tangy, rich and creamy taste. Low-fat buttermilk has the same amount of fat as low-fat milk.

1 tbsp	olive or safflower oil	15 ml
1	large onion, chopped	1
2	cloves garlic, minced	2
1	leek, white and light part only	1
2	stalks celery, chopped	2
1	large potato, peeled and diced	1
2 cups	low-sodium chicken or vegetable stock	500 ml
2 cups	water	500 ml
2 cups	watercress, chopped	500 ml
2 cups	chopped fresh spinach	500 ml
¾ cup	low-fat buttermilk or milk	175 ml
	sea salt and freshly ground pepper to taste	
Garnish:	croutons (optional)	

1. In a large saucepan, heat oil over medium heat. Add onion, garlic, leek and celery; sauté for 4 minutes.
2. Add potato, stock, water, watercress and spinach; bring to a boil. Reduce heat, cover and simmer for 15 minutes. Remove from heat and cool slightly.
3. Purée soup in the saucepan using an immersion blender or transfer in batches to a blender or food processor and blend until smooth. Return soup to saucepan, add buttermilk or milk and simmer until heated. Do not boil. Season with salt and pepper and serve garnished with croutons, if desired.

⤖ Tip: This soup is also delicious served chilled. For a thinner consistency, add extra water or stock.

Poultry & Meat Soups

Capture the Abundance of Flavour

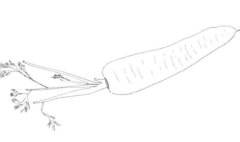

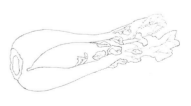

All our yesterdays are summerized in our now,
and all our tomorrows are ours to shape.

Hal Borland

African Peanut Chicken Soup

Serves 6 to 8

*On a recent family holiday we stayed at a wonderful
little hotel in Cape Town, South Africa. Just down the
road, we visited a small family-owned restaurant where
I was introduced to the unusual combination of chicken,
sweet potatoes and peanuts.*

2 tbsp	olive or safflower oil	25 ml
1	large onion, chopped	1
4	cloves garlic, minced	4
1	sweet green pepper, chopped	1
1 lb	boneless, skinless chicken breasts, cubed	500 g
2 tsp	grated fresh gingerroot	10 ml
2 tsp	chili powder	10 ml
2 cups	low-sodium chicken or vegetable stock	500 ml
3 cups	water	750 ml
1 cup	tomato juice	250 ml
1	sweet potato, peeled and cubed	1
1	baking potato, peeled and cubed	1
1 cup	fresh or frozen corn kernels	250 ml
¼ cup	peanut butter	50 ml
	dash hot pepper sauce or to taste	
Garnish:	chopped peanuts (optional)	
	chopped green onions	

1. In a large saucepan, heat oil over medium heat. Add onion, garlic and
   green pepper; sauté for 4 minutes. Add chicken, gingerroot and chili
   powder; sauté for 3 minutes longer.
2. Add stock, water, tomato juice, sweet potato, baking potato and corn;
   bring to a boil. Reduce heat, cover and simmer for 20 minutes or until
   potatoes are tender, stirring occasionally. Remove from heat, stir in
   peanut butter until well blended and season with hot pepper sauce. Serve
   garnished with chopped peanuts, if desired, and green onions.

Chicken Wonton Soup

Serves 6 to 8

*Don't be intimidated by the thought of making
wontons. They are easy to make and well worth
the extra little effort.*

Wontons

¹⁄₂ lb	lean ground chicken	250 g
1 tsp	finely grated fresh gingerroot	5 ml
1 tsp	low-sodium soy sauce	5 ml
1 tsp	cornstarch	5 ml
¹⁄₂ tsp	sesame oil	2 ml
2 tbsp	finely grated carrot	25 ml
1 tbsp	finely chopped green onion	15 ml
1	egg white, lightly beaten	1
24	wonton wrappers	24

1. Combine chicken, gingerroot, soy sauce, cornstarch, sesame oil, carrot
    and green onion.
2. Moisten edges of wonton wrappers with egg white. Place 1 tsp/5 ml of
    mixture onto the centre of each wrapper. Pull the top corner down to
    meet the bottom, folding the wrapper over the filling to make a triangle.
    Press edges to make a seal. Bring left and right corners together above
    the filling. Overlap the tips, moisten with egg white and press together to
    make a purse shape. Set aside.

For the Love of Soup

Soup

3 cups	low-sodium chicken stock	750 ml
3 cups	water	750 ml
2 tbsp	fresh lemon juice	25 ml
1 tbsp	low-sodium soy sauce	15 ml
	dash hot pepper sauce or to taste	
2	green onions, chopped	2
2	small carrots, scraped and sliced diagonally	2
1 cup	snow peas, halved diagonally	250 ml

Combine stock, water, lemon juice, soy sauce and hot sauce in a large saucepan; bring to a boil.

Add green onions, carrots, snow peas and wontons; simmer for 4 minutes or until wontons are tender. To ensure that the chicken is cooked, remove one wonton, cut it in half and check that the filling is no longer pink.

Cajun Chicken Soup

Serves 4 to 6

This is my version of a Cajun-style gumbo. It is much lighter than the traditional stew and the hot pepper sauce can be increased (or decreased) depending on your palate.

2 tbsp	olive or safflower oil	25 ml
1	onion, chopped	1
3	cloves garlic, minced	3
1	sweet green pepper, chopped	1
1 lb	skinless, boneless chicken breast, cubed	500 g
2 cups	low-sodium chicken or vegetable stock	500 ml
2 cups	water	500 ml
1	can (19 oz/540 ml) diced tomatoes	1
¼ cup	long-grain rice	50 ml
2 cups	fresh or frozen corn kernels	500 ml
1 cup	sliced frozen okra or peas, partially thawed	250 ml
1 tbsp	fresh lemon juice	15 ml
1 tbsp	chopped fresh thyme or 1 tsp/5 ml dried thyme	15 ml
2 tsp	chopped fresh oregano or ½ tsp/2 ml dried oregano	10 ml
2 tsp	paprika	10 ml
1 tsp	celery seeds	5 ml
	dash hot pepper sauce or to taste	
	sea salt and freshly ground pepper to taste	
Garnish:	chopped fresh cilantro or Italian parsley	

1. In a large saucepan, heat oil over medium heat. Add onion, garlic and green pepper; sauté for 4 minutes. Stir in chicken and cook for 3 minutes longer.
2. Add stock, water, tomatoes with juice, rice, corn, okra or peas, lemon juice, thyme, oregano, paprika, celery seeds and hot pepper sauce; bring to a boil. Reduce heat, cover and simmer for 20 minutes or until rice is tender, stirring occasionally. Season with salt and pepper and serve garnished with cilantro or parsley.

For the Love of Soup

Corn & Chicken Chowder

Serves 4 to 6

A light and tasty chowder that is easy to prepare.

1 tbsp	unsalted butter	15 ml
1 tbsp	olive or safflower oil	15 ml
2	large leeks, white and light parts only, chopped	2
1	stalk celery, chopped	1
2	baking potatoes, peeled and diced	2
2 cups	low-sodium chicken or vegetable stock	500 ml
1 cup	water	250 ml
2 cups	fresh or frozen corn kernels	500 ml
2 tsp	chopped fresh thyme or ½ tsp/2 ml dried	10 ml
2 cups	diced cooked chicken	500 ml
1 cup	low-fat milk	250 ml
2	green onions, sliced	2
2 tbsp	chopped fresh Italian parsley	25 ml
	sea salt and freshly ground pepper to taste	

1. In a large saucepan, heat butter and oil over medium heat. Add leeks and celery; sauté for 6 minutes. Stir in potatoes and sauté for 4 minutes longer.
2. Add stock, water, corn and thyme; bring to a boil. Reduce heat, cover and simmer for 10 minutes. Remove from heat.
3. Partially purée soup in saucepan using an immersion blender or transfer 2 cups/500 ml to a blender or food processor and blend until smooth. Return puréed portion back into the saucepan.
4. Add chicken, milk, green onions and parsley; simmer until heated and season with salt and pepper.

Hot & Sour Chicken Soup

Serves 4 to 6

*The fascinating city of Hong Kong was one of my
favourite destinations. I recall having a hot and sour
chicken soup in Kowloon that was absolutely delicious.
This is my re-creation of that memorable soup. Enjoy!*

4 cups	low-sodium chicken stock	1 L
2 cups	water	500 ml
8 oz	skinless, boneless chicken pieces, sliced	250 g
1	small onion, slivered	1
2	cloves garlic, minced	2
2 tsp	grated fresh gingerroot	10 ml
2	carrots, scraped and sliced	2
2 cups	thinly sliced mushrooms	500 ml
2 cups	chopped bok choy or napa cabbage	500 ml
1 cup	frozen peas, partially thawed	250 ml
4 oz	firm tofu, cubed	125 g
2 tbsp	low-sodium soy sauce	25 ml
2 tbsp	rice vinegar	25 ml
	hot pepper sauce to taste	
2 tbsp	cornstarch	25 ml
	(dissolved in ⅓ cup/80 ml water)	
2	eggs, lightly beaten	2
2	green onions, thinly sliced	2

1. In a large saucepan, bring stock and water to a boil. Add chicken, onion, garlic, gingerroot, carrots, mushrooms, bok choy or cabbage, peas, tofu, soy sauce, vinegar and hot pepper sauce; reduce heat and simmer for 8 minutes.

2. Stir in cornstarch mixture; reduce heat and simmer for 4 minutes or until the soup starts to thicken slightly. Gradually add the beaten eggs in a slow stream, stirring constantly. Remove from heat and stir in green onions.

⤷ Tip: For a vegetarian version of this soup, use extra tofu and vegetable stock in place of chicken and chicken stock.

For the Love of Soup

Corn, Wild Rice & Barley Soup with Black Forest Ham

Serves 6 to 8

This robust soup is a taste delight. The wonderful consistency and flavour of corn, wild rice and barley come alive with the smoky flavour of the ham.

½ cup	wild rice	125 ml
¼ cup	barley	50 ml
3 cups	water	750 ml
1 tbsp	olive or safflower oil	15 ml
1	onion, finely chopped	1
1	stalk celery, diced	1
1	carrot, scraped and diced	1
3 cups	fresh or frozen corn kernels	750 ml
2 cups	low-sodium chicken or vegetable stock	500 ml
2 cups	water	500 ml
1	bay leaf	1
4 oz	black forest ham, diced	125 g
1 cup	low-fat milk	250 ml
	sea salt and freshly ground pepper to taste	
Garnish:	chopped fresh Italian parsley or chives	

1. Place rice, barley and water in a medium-sized saucepan; bring to a boil. Reduce heat, cover and simmer for 45 minutes or until rice is cooked, stirring occasionally.
2. Meanwhile, in large saucepan, heat oil over medium heat. Add onion, celery and carrot; sauté for 4 minutes. Add corn, stock, water and bay leaf; bring to a boil. Reduce heat, cover and simmer for 10 minutes. Remove from heat and cool slightly. Discard bay leaf.
3. Partially purée soup in saucepan using an immersion blender or transfer 2 cups/500 ml of the soup to a blender or food processor and blend until smooth. Return puréed portion back into the saucepan. Add rice and barley, ham and milk; simmer for 10 minutes. Do not boil. Season with salt and pepper and serve garnished with parsley or chives.

Matzo Ball Soup

Serves 6 to 8

I love matzo ball soup! I crave this soup the moment the aroma of my homemade stock permeates the air. On a cool winter day this soup is guaranteed to comfort you.

Matzo Balls

3	large eggs	3
3 tbsp	safflower oil	50 ml
¾ cup	matzo meal	175 ml
½ tsp	sea salt	2 ml
1 tbsp	finely chopped fresh parsley	15 ml
3 tbsp	water	50 ml

1. In a medium bowl beat the eggs, add the oil and beat again. Stir in the matzo meal, salt and parsley and blend in the water. Cover the dough and refrigerate for at least 15 minutes.

2. In a large saucepan, bring 6 cups/1.5 L water to a boil. With moistened hands, shape the matzo mixture into 1-inch /2.5-cm balls and drop into the boiling water. Partially cover the saucepan and cook over medium heat for 20 minutes. Drain the liquid and let the matzo balls cool to room temperature. Refrigerate until ready to add to the soup.

Soup

1 tbsp	safflower oil	15 ml
1	small onion, finely chopped	1
1	leek, white and light part only, finely chopped	1
2	cloves garlic, minced	2
6 cups	low-sodium chicken stock (preferably homemade)	1.5 L
2 cups	water	500 ml
2	stalks celery, thinly sliced	2
2	carrots, scraped and thinly sliced	2
2	parsnips, scraped and thinly sliced	2
1	bay leaf	1
2 tbsp	chopped fresh Italian parsley	25 ml
	sea salt and freshly ground pepper to taste	

1. In a large saucepan, heat oil over medium heat. Add onion, leek and garlic; sauté for 4 minutes.
2. Add stock, water, celery, carrots, parsnips and bay leaf; bring to a boil. Reduce heat, cover and simmer for 20 minutes.
3. Add parsley and matzo balls; simmer for 5 minutes or until heated. Remove bay leaf and season with salt and pepper.

Mexican-Style Turkey Meatball Soup

Serves 4 to 6

This soup is wonderful for a casual après-ski meal. Serve with a crusty loaf of fresh bread or cornbread.

Meatballs

	oil or non-stick cooking spray for baking sheet	
1 lb	lean ground turkey or chicken	500 g
½ cup	quick cooking oats	125 ml
2	cloves garlic, minced	2
½ tsp	ground cumin	2 ml
2 tbsp	finely chopped fresh cilantro or parsley	25 ml
1	egg, slightly beaten	1
	sea salt and freshly ground pepper to taste	

Preheat oven to 350°F/180°C.

1. Rub a small amount of oil or use non-stick cooking spray on a baking sheet.
2. In a bowl, combine all other ingredients well. Shape meat mixture into 1-inch/2.5-cm balls. Place meatballs on baking sheet and bake for 15 minutes. Drain on paper towels and set aside.

> ↩ Tip: Dampen your hands or rub them with a little oil before rolling meatballs to prevent meat from sticking.

Microwave directions:

Place half of the meatballs on a microwave dish and cover with waxed paper. Cook on medium heat for 4 to 6 minutes or until no longer pink. Remove from plate and repeat with remaining meatballs. Drain on paper towels and set aside.

Soup

1 tbsp	olive or safflower oil	15 ml
1	large onion, chopped	1
2	cloves garlic, minced	2
2	carrots, scraped and diced	2
2	stalks celery, diced	2
1	jalapeno pepper, seeded and minced	1
2 tsp	chili powder	10 ml
1 tsp	ground cumin	5 ml
1 tsp	chopped fresh oregano	5 ml
	or $\frac{1}{2}$ tsp/2 ml dried oregano	
1	can (28 oz/796 ml) stewed tomatoes, chopped	1
3 cups	low-sodium chicken or vegetable stock	750 ml
3 cups	water	750 ml
	sea salt and freshly ground pepper to taste	

Garnish:	diced avocado	
	chopped fresh cilantro or Italian parsley	

1. In a large saucepan, heat oil over medium heat. Add onion, garlic, carrots, celery and jalapeno pepper; sauté for 4 minutes. Stir in chili powder, cumin and oregano; sauté for 1 minute longer
2. Add tomatoes with juice, stock, water and meatballs; bring to a boil. Reduce heat, cover and simmer for 20 minutes, stirring occasionally. Season with salt and pepper. Serve garnished with avocado and cilantro.

Mom's Chicken & Rice Soup

Serves 4 to 6

The aroma of this comforting soup takes me back to those snowy winters in New Brunswick when my mother often prepared it for our Sunday meal. The soup had many variations; sometimes noodles replaced the rice, and whatever vegetable was on hand went into the pot. I love my Mom.

1 tbsp	unsalted butter	15 ml
1 tbsp	olive or safflower oil	15 ml
2	leeks, white and light green parts only, sliced	2
1	onion, chopped	1
2	stalks celery, sliced	2
4 cups	low-sodium chicken stock	1 L
4 cups	water	1 L
½ cup	white wine (optional)	125 ml
2	bone-in chicken legs or bone-in chicken breast pieces, skin removed	2
2	bay leaves	2
1 tsp	chopped fresh thyme or ¼ tsp/1 ml dried thyme	5 ml
⅓ cup	long-grain rice	80 ml
2	carrots, scraped and sliced	2
½ cup	frozen peas, partially thawed	125 ml
¼ cup	chopped fresh Italian parsley	50 ml
	sea salt and freshly ground pepper to taste	

1. In a large saucepan, heat butter and oil over medium heat. Add leeks, onion and celery; sauté for 4 minutes. Add stock and water, wine if desired, chicken pieces, bay leaves and thyme; bring to a boil. Reduce heat, cover and simmer for 40 minutes. Remove from heat.
2. Remove chicken pieces from the saucepan and place on a cutting board. When cool enough to handle, remove meat from bones and discard bones. Cut chicken in bite-sized pieces and return to saucepan.
3. Add rice, carrots and peas; cover and simmer for 20 minutes or until rice is tender. Discard bay leaves.
4. Stir in parsley and season with salt and pepper.

> ✎ Tip: One large onion can be used to replace leeks. If substituting noodles for rice add 1 cup/250 ml of dried noodles and cook for 10 minutes or until tender but firm.

Chicken, Shiitake & Noodle Soup

Serves 6 to 8

In Asia I was served a version of this soup with a scoop-shaped spoon for the broth and chopsticks for the noodles. No matter how you choose to eat it, you'll find this soup's tantalizing combination of flavours impossible to resist.

1 pkg	fresh udon noodles (14 oz/400 g)	1
1 tbsp	safflower oil	15 ml
1	small onion, diced	1
2	cloves garlic, minced	2
8	medium shiitake mushrooms, thinly sliced, stems discarded	8
1 tbsp	grated fresh gingerroot	15 ml
1 lb	boneless, skinless chicken breast, cubed	500 g
4 cups	low-sodium chicken or vegetable stock	1 L
4 cups	water	1 L
1 tbsp	miso paste	15 ml
1 tbsp	low-sodium soy sauce	15 ml
1 tbsp	fish sauce	15 ml
1 tsp	sugar	5 ml
2 cups	bok choy or napa cabbage, thinly sliced	500 ml
2	carrots, scraped and thinly sliced	2
4	green onions, thinly sliced	4
	freshly ground pepper to taste	

1. Cook noodles in boiling water for 3 minutes or until almost tender. Rinse in cold water and drain well. Set aside.
2. In a large saucepan, heat oil over medium heat. Add onion, garlic, mushrooms, gingerroot and chicken; sauté for 4 minutes.
3. Add stock, water, miso paste, soy sauce, fish sauce and sugar; bring to a boil. Reduce heat and simmer for 10 minutes. Add bok choy, carrots, green onions and noodles; cook for 3 minutes and season with pepper.

⮌ Tip: Miso paste, udon noodles and fish sauce can be found in Asian markets and well-stocked supermarkets. Fettuccine and linguine are both good substitutes for udon noodles.

Turkey Vegetable Chili Soup

This soup has all the ingredients of a chili but with fewer beans, more broth and lots of vegetables. This is a soup you definitely want to prepare early in the day (or even the day before) to give the flavours time to blend. Like all hearty soups, it tastes even better reheated.

2 tbsp	olive or safflower oil	25 ml
1 lb	lean ground turkey or chicken	500 g
1	onion, chopped	1
4	cloves garlic, minced	4
2	stalks celery, chopped	2
1	sweet green or red pepper, chopped	1
2	carrots, scraped, cut in half and sliced	2
½ tsp	ground cumin	2 ml
1 tbsp	chili powder	15 ml
1 tbsp	chopped fresh oregano	15 ml
	or 1 tsp/5 ml dried oregano	
½ tsp	hot chili flakes or to taste	2 ml
2 cups	low-sodium chicken or vegetable stock	500 ml
2 cups	water	500 ml
2 tbsp	tomato paste	25 ml
1	can (28 oz/796 ml) tomatoes, chopped	1
1	can (19 oz/540 ml) red kidney beans,	1
	drained and rinsed	
1 cup	fresh or frozen corn kernels	250 ml
1	medium zucchini, cut in half and sliced	1
	sea salt to taste	
Garnish:	chopped fresh cilantro or Italian parsley	
	low-fat sour cream (optional)	

1. In a large saucepan, heat 1 tbsp/15 ml of oil over medium heat. Add turkey, cook until no longer pink, about 5 minutes, breaking up with the back of a spoon. Drain off any fat.
2. Add remaining oil, onion, garlic, celery, green or red pepper and carrots; sauté for 4 minutes. Stir in cumin, chili powder, oregano and chili flakes and cook for 2 minutes longer.
3. Add stock, water, tomato paste and tomatoes with juice; bring to a boil. Reduce heat, cover and simmer for 30 minutes, stirring occasionally.
4. Add beans, corn and zucchini and simmer for 15 minutes longer. Season with salt to taste and serve garnished with cilantro and sour cream, if desired.

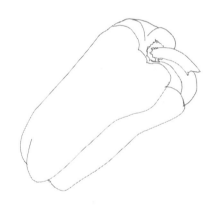

Mulligatawny Soup

Serves 6 to 8

A little Indian restaurant in the multicultural city of Amsterdam was the first place I ever tried this world-renowned soup. Mulligatawny (chicken curry soup) is peppery and has a hint of fruitiness.

2 tbsp	safflower oil	25 ml
1	medium red onion, chopped	1
3	cloves garlic, minced	3
2	stalks celery, diced	2
1 lb	skinless, boneless chicken pieces, cubed	500 g
2 tsp	mild curry paste	10 ml
1 tsp	grated fresh gingerroot	5 ml
2 cups	low-sodium chicken or vegetable stock	500 ml
4 cups	water	1 L
2	carrots, scraped and diced	2
2 cups	peeled, diced turnip or rutabaga	500 ml
2	tart apples, peeled, cored and diced	2
1	bay leaf	1
	dash hot pepper sauce or to taste	
⅓ cup	long-grain white rice	80 ml
1 cup	fresh or canned tomatoes, diced	250 ml
	sea salt and freshly ground pepper to taste	
Garnish:	chopped fresh Italian parsley	
	low-fat sour cream or yogurt (optional)	

1. In a large saucepan, heat oil over medium heat. Add onion, garlic and celery; sauté for 4 minutes. Add chicken, curry and gingerroot; sauté for 2 minutes longer.
2. Add stock and water, carrots, turnip, apples, bay leaf, hot pepper sauce, rice and tomato; bring to a boil. Reduce heat, cover and simmer for 20 minutes, stirring occasionally. Remove bay leaf and season with salt and pepper. Serve garnished with parsley and a dollop of sour cream or yogurt, if desired.

Chicken Soup
with Lime & Cilantro

Serves 4 to 6

*If I had to choose one soup to eat on a regular basis,
this would be the one. The combination of cilantro, which
has a pleasant pungent taste, and the lime juice, makes
this soup refreshing even on a hot day.*

1 tbsp	olive or safflower oil	15 ml
1	medium onion, chopped	1
2	cloves garlic, minced	2
2 tsp	chili powder	10 ml
3	skinless, boneless chicken breast pieces, diced	3
2 cups	low-sodium chicken or vegetable stock	500 ml
2 cups	water	500 ml
2	ripe tomatoes, chopped	2
1 cup	fresh or frozen corn kernels	250 ml
¼ cup	fresh lime juice	50 ml
	small bunch fresh cilantro sprigs, tied together with kitchen string	
	sea salt and freshly ground pepper	
Garnish:	chopped fresh cilantro	

1. In a large saucepan, heat oil over medium heat. Add onion and garlic; sauté for 4 minutes. Add chili powder and chicken; sauté for 2 minutes longer.
2. Add stock, water, tomatoes, corn, lime juice and cilantro sprigs; bring to a boil. Reduce heat, cover and simmer for 15 minutes. Remove and discard cilantro sprigs. Season with salt and pepper and serve garnished with fresh cilantro.

Turkey Barley Soup

I used to think that if you wanted to enjoy a turkey soup, you had to wait for Thanksgiving leftovers. These days, you can find turkey breasts at the supermarket and make up a batch of this wholesome soup anytime the craving hits.

1 tbsp	olive or safflower oil	15 ml
2	leeks, white and light green parts only, sliced	2
2	cloves garlic, minced	2
2	stalks celery, sliced	2
3 cups	low-sodium chicken stock	750 ml
3 cups	water	750 ml
1 lb	skinless, bone-in turkey breast	500 g
1/3 cup	pearl barley	80 ml
2	carrots, scraped and sliced	2
1 tbsp	chopped fresh thyme or 1 tsp/5 ml dried thyme	15 ml
1 tsp	Worcestershire sauce	5 ml
1	can (19 oz/540 ml) tomatoes, chopped	1
2	small zucchini, sliced	2
2 tbsp	chopped fresh Italian parsley sea salt and freshly ground pepper to taste	25 ml

1. In a large saucepan, heat oil over medium heat. Add leeks, garlic and celery; sauté for 4 minutes.
2. Add stock and water, turkey breast, barley, carrots, thyme and Worcestershire sauce; bring to a boil. Reduce heat, cover and simmer for 45 minutes, stirring occasionally. Remove turkey breast from the saucepan and place on a cutting board. When cool enough to handle, remove turkey meat from the bones and discard the bones; dice turkey and return to saucepan.
3. Add tomatoes with juice, zucchini and parsley; simmer for 5 minutes until heated and barley is tender. Season with sea salt and pepper.

Chunky Potato Leek Soup
with Black Forest Ham

Serves 4 to 6

The smoky taste of ham and the wonderful essence of sage combine to bring out the subtle flavours in this soup.

1 tbsp	unsalted butter	15 ml
2	leeks, white and light parts only, thinly sliced	2
2	stalks celery, finely sliced	2
2 cups	low-sodium chicken or vegetable stock	250 ml
2 cups	water	250 ml
1	baking potato, peeled and diced	1
4	small red potatoes, scrubbed and diced	4
1	bay leaf	1
2 tsp	finely chopped fresh sage or ½ tsp/2 ml dried sage	10 ml
2 tbsp	finely chopped fresh Italian parsley	25 ml
4 oz	Black Forest ham, diced	125 g
1 cup	low-fat milk	250 ml
	sea salt and freshly ground pepper to taste	

1. In a large saucepan, melt butter over medium heat. Add leeks and celery; sauté for 6 minutes. Add stock and water, potatoes, bay leaf and sage; bring to a boil. Reduce heat; cover and simmer for 15 minutes or until potatoes are tender, stirring occasionally. Remove from heat and discard bay leaf.
2. Partially purée soup in saucepan using an immersion blender or transfer 2 cups/500 ml to a blender or food processor and blend until smooth; return puréed portion back into the saucepan. Add parsley, ham and milk; simmer until heated and season with salt and pepper. Do not boil.

French Canadian Pea Soup

Serves 8

This classic soup was a staple at my childhood home in Grand Falls, New Brunswick. It is nutritious, hearty and economical. Make the soup ahead of time; it will become creamier and thicker as it sits.

2 cups	dried yellow split peas	500 ml
12 cups	water	3 L
1 tbsp	unsalted butter	15 ml
1	large onion, finely chopped	1
1	stalk celery, finely chopped	1
2	carrots, scraped and finely chopped	2
2 cups	low-sodium chicken or vegetable stock	500 ml
6 cups	water	1.5 L
4 oz	lean smoked ham, diced	125 g
1 tsp	chopped fresh thyme, or ¼ tsp/1 ml dried thyme	5 ml
1	bay leaf	1
	sea salt and freshly ground pepper to taste	

1. Place peas in a saucepan and cover with 12 cups/3 L of water; bring to a boil and cook for 6 minutes. Drain and rinse the peas, set aside.
2. In a large saucepan, melt butter over medium heat. Add onion, celery and carrots; sauté for 4 minutes.
3. Add stock and water, ham, thyme, bay leaf and peas; bring to a boil. Reduce heat, cover and simmer for 50 minutes to 1 hour, or until peas are very soft; stir occasionally. Remove bay leaf and season with salt and pepper.

> Tip: Instead of using a ham bone, which the traditional recipe calls for, I like to use a small amount of lean smoked ham. This is a leaner alternative.

Asian-Style Beef & Vegetable Soup

Serves 4 to 6

This aromatic soup is delicious and satisfying.

1 tbsp	sesame oil	15 ml
12 oz	sirloin beef, sliced thinly	375 g
1 tbsp	safflower oil	15 ml
2	onions, halved and thinly sliced	2
2	cloves garlic, minced	2
2 tsp	grated fresh gingerroot	10 ml
¼ cup	long-grain rice	50 ml
2 cups	low-sodium beef stock	500 ml
2 cups	water	500 ml
2 cups	chopped bok choy or napa cabbage	500 ml
2	large ripe tomatoes, chopped	2
2 tbsp	dark miso	25 ml
2 tbsp	cornstarch	25 ml
	(dissolved in ⅓ cup/80 ml water)	

1. In a large saucepan, heat sesame oil over medium heat. Stir-fry the beef for 1 to 2 minutes, just until browned. Transfer to a plate and set aside.
2. Heat safflower oil in saucepan over medium heat. Add onions and garlic; sauté for 4 minutes. Stir in gingerroot and rice and cook for 2 minutes longer.
3. Add stock and water, cabbage and tomatoes; bring to a boil. Reduce heat, cover and simmer for 15 minutes or until rice is tender.
4. In a small bowl, combine miso with cornstarch and water; add mixture to soup and simmer until slightly thickened, about 5 minutes. Add reserved beef just before serving.

⤶ Tip: Chill meat in freezer for 20 minutes, or until firm but not frozen. This will make it easier to slice.

Beef Goulash Soup with Noodles

Serves 4 to 6

The perfect end to a long day is a delicious, nutritious hearty soup, ready to eat. Remember to simmer just until heated to be sure not to overcook the noodles. Before reheating you may need to thin the broth with a little water or tomato juice.

2 tbsp	olive or safflower oil	25 ml
12 oz	lean ground beef	375 g
1	onion, chopped	1
3	cloves garlic, minced	3
2	stalks celery, sliced	2
2	carrots, scraped and sliced	2
1	sweet red pepper, chopped	1
2 cups	low-sodium beef stock	500 ml
2 cups	water	500 ml
1 tbsp	chopped fresh oregano	15 ml
	or 1 tsp/5 ml dried oregano	
¼ tsp	caraway seeds	1 ml
2 tsp	paprika	10 ml
½ cup	dry red wine (optional)	125 ml
1 tbsp	balsamic vinegar	15 ml
1 cup	tomato juice	250 ml
1 cup	frozen peas, partially thawed	250 ml
1½ cups	broad egg noodles	375 ml
	sea salt and freshly ground pepper to taste	

1. In a large saucepan, heat 1 tbsp/15 ml of oil over medium heat. Add beef and cook for about 4 minutes, or until it is no longer pink, breaking it up with a wooden spoon. Drain off fat and transfer meat to a plate.
2. Heat remaining oil in saucepan. Add onion, garlic and celery; sauté for 4 minutes. Return meat to saucepan and add carrots, red pepper, stock and water, oregano, caraway seeds, paprika, red wine, vinegar, tomato juice and peas; bring to a boil. Reduce heat, cover and simmer for 15 minutes.
3. Bring to a gentle boil and stir in egg noodles. Cook uncovered for 8 to 10 minutes or until noodles are tender but firm. Season with salt and pepper.

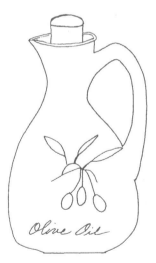

Olive Oil

Country-Style Beef Vegetable Soup

Serves 6 to 8

This aromatic tasty soup is a revised version of Quebec's pot-au-feu, which means pot over fire in French. It takes a little extra time to prepare but is well worth it.

2 lbs	meaty beef short ribs cut into chunks (trim off any visible fat)	1 kg
8 cups	water	2 L
2 cups	low-sodium beef stock	500 ml
2	sprigs of thyme	2
2	bay leaves	2
2 tbsp	olive or safflower oil	25 ml
2	onions, chopped	2
2	cloves garlic, minced	2
2	stalks celery, sliced	2
2 cups	tomato juice	500 ml
2 tbsp	tomato paste	25 ml
2	carrots, scraped, and sliced	2
2	potatoes, peeled and cubed	2
2	parsnips, peeled and sliced	2
2 cups	chopped Savoy cabbage	500 ml
2 cups	cubed, peeled turnip or rutabaga	500 ml
1 cup	frozen green peas, partially thawed	250 ml
	sea salt and freshly ground pepper to taste	

For the Love of Soup

1. In a large saucepan combine ribs, water, stock, thyme and bay leaves and bring to a boil. Reduce heat and simmer for 1 hour. Skim off any froth that rises to the surface.
2. Remove from heat and strain through a fine sieve into a large bowl. Let ribs cool for a few minutes then remove meat from bones, cut into bite-sized pieces and discard bones, thyme and bay leaves. Set beef and broth aside.
3. In saucepan, heat oil over medium heat. Add onions, garlic and celery; sauté for 4 minutes. Add reserved beef and broth, tomato juice, tomato paste, carrots, potatoes, parsnips, cabbage, turnip and peas; bring to a boil. Reduce heat; cover and simmer for 30 minutes or until vegetables are tender, stirring occasionally.
4. Set aside for 15 minutes to allow any fat from the meat to rise to the surface. Carefully remove the layer of fat with a shallow metal spoon. Season with salt and pepper.

> ↪ Tip: Making this soup ahead of time and refrigerating will allow the fat from the meat to solidify so it's easier to remove. This method will guarantee you a low-fat soup.

Hamburger Soup

Serves 8

This beef and barley soup is a favourite for winter warmth. I reduced the sodium and increased the veggies to make it a healthier version.

2 tbsp	olive or safflower oil	25 ml
1 lb	lean ground beef	500 g
1	onion, chopped	1
3	cloves garlic, minced	3
3 cups	sliced mushrooms	750 ml
2	stalks celery, chopped	2
3 cups	low-sodium beef stock	750 ml
3 cups	water	750 ml
2	carrots, scraped and chopped	2
1	large potato, peeled and diced	1
2 cups	peeled, diced turnip or rutabaga	500 ml
2 tsp	chopped fresh thyme	10 ml
	or ½ tsp/2 ml dried thyme	
2 tbsp	chopped fresh Italian parsley	25 ml
½ cup	barley	125 ml
1	can (28 oz/796 ml) tomatoes, chopped	1
½ cup	red wine	125 ml
1 tbsp	Worcestershire sauce	15 ml
	sea salt and freshly ground pepper to taste	

1. In a large saucepan, heat 1 tbsp/15 ml of oil over medium heat. Add ground beef and sauté for 5 minutes or until meat is no longer pink. Drain and set aside.
2. Heat remaining oil in saucepan. Add onion, garlic, mushrooms and celery; sauté for 4 minutes.
3. Return beef to saucepan. Add stock and water, carrots, potato, turnip, thyme, parsley, barley, tomatoes with juice, red wine and Worcestershire sauce; bring to a boil. Reduce heat, cover and simmer for 30 minutes or until barley is tender; stir occasionally. Season with salt and pepper.

Hearty Lamb & Bean Soup with Port

Serve 6 to 8

My husband Tim loves lamb so this soup is one of his favourites. It is a nourishing and tasty meal-in-a-bowl.

2 tbsp	olive oil	25 ml
1 lb	lean boneless lamb, cut into bite-sized pieces	500 g
1	onion, chopped	1
4	cloves garlic, minced	4
1	sweet green or red pepper, chopped	1
2 cups	low-sodium beef stock	500 ml
3 cups	water	750 ml
1	can (28 oz/796 ml) tomatoes, chopped	1
2	carrots, scraped and sliced	2
1	large potato, peeled and diced	1
1 tbsp	chopped fresh oregano or 1 tsp/5 ml dried oregano	15 ml
1 tbsp	chopped fresh rosemary or 1 tsp/5 ml dried rosemary	15 ml
1/3 cup	port wine	80 ml
2 cups	white kidney beans or chickpeas, cooked or canned (drained and rinsed) sea salt and freshly ground pepper to taste	500 ml
Garnish:	chopped fresh Italian parsley	

1. In a large saucepan, heat 1 tbsp/15 ml of oil over medium-high heat; add lamb and brown, in batches if necessary. Drain off fat and transfer meat to a plate.
2. Heat remaining oil in saucepan, add onion, garlic and green or red pepper; sauté for 3 minutes.
3. Return lamb to saucepan and add stock and water, tomatoes with juice, carrots, potato, oregano, rosemary, port and beans; bring to a boil. Reduce heat, cover and simmer for 30 minutes, stirring occasionally. Remove bay leaf, season with salt and pepper and serve garnished with a sprinkle of chopped parsley.

Hearty Portuguese Bean Soup

Serves 8

My very first overseas trip was to Lisbon. I had a bowl of creamy bean soup that was out of this world. I thought the thickness came from cream, but the chef at Maria's Restaurant taught me that her secret was to purée part of the soup.

4 oz	Spanish chorizo or kielbasa, diced	125 g
1 tbsp	olive oil	15 ml
1	onion, chopped	1
2	leeks, white and light parts only, chopped	2
3	cloves garlic, minced	3
2	carrots, scraped and sliced	2
2 cups	peeled, diced turnip or rutabaga	500 ml
4 cups	coarsely chopped Savoy cabbage	1 L
1	bay leaf	1
2 cups	low-sodium chicken or vegetable stock	500 ml
4 cups	water	1 L
4 cups	white kidney beans, cooked or canned (drained and rinsed)	1 L
	sea salt and freshly ground pepper to taste	

1. In a large saucepan over medium heat, sauté chorizo or kielbasa until it is lightly browned and transfer it with a slotted spoon to paper towels to drain.

2. In a large saucepan, heat oil over medium heat. Add onion, leeks and garlic; sauté for 4 minutes. Add carrots, turnip or rutabaga, cabbage, bay leaf, stock, water, beans and chorizo or kielbasa; bring to a boil. Reduce heat, cover and simmer for 30 minutes, stirring occasionally. Remove bay leaf and season with salt and pepper.

3. Partially purée soup in saucepan using an immersion blender or transfer 2 cups/500 ml to a blender or food processor and blend until smooth. Return puréed portion back into the saucepan and simmer soup until heated.

↩ Tip: Because the chorizo or kielbasa adds its own salty flavour, go light on the salt, but use ample ground pepper.

For the Love of Soup

Italian Beef & Bean Soup

Serves 8

A colourful, robust soup that is perfect for lunch. All you need is salad and fresh crusty bread.

2 tbsp	olive oil	25 ml
12 oz	lean ground beef	375 g
1	onion, chopped	1
4	cloves garlic, minced	4
2	stalks celery, chopped	2
2	carrots, scraped and chopped	2
3 cups	quartered mushrooms	750 ml
3 cups	low-sodium beef stock	750 ml
3 cups	water	750 ml
2	bay leaves	2
3 tbsp	fresh basil, chopped	50 ml
	or 1 tbsp/15 ml dried basil	
1 tbsp	chopped fresh oregano	15 ml
	or 1 tsp/5 ml dried oregano	
¼ tsp	hot chili flakes or to taste	1 ml
2 cups	chopped Savoy cabbage	500 ml
1	can (28 oz/796 ml) plum tomatoes, chopped	1
2 tbsp	tomato paste	25 ml
1	can (19 oz/540 ml) chickpeas or kidney beans, drained and rinsed	1
Garnish:	grated fresh Parmesan cheese (optional)	

1. In a large saucepan, heat 1 tbsp/15 ml of oil over medium heat. Add beef and cook, breaking up meat with a wooden spoon, for about 4 minutes or until meat is no longer pink. Drain off fat and transfer meat to a plate.
2. Heat remaining oil in saucepan and add onion, garlic, celery, carrots and mushrooms; sauté for 4 minutes.
3. Return meat to saucepan and add stock and water, bay leaves, basil, oregano, chili flakes, cabbage, tomatoes with juice, tomato paste and beans; bring to a boil. Reduce heat, cover and simmer for 30 minutes, stirring occasionally. Serve with Parmesan cheese, if desired.

Italian Pasta & Bean Soup

Serves 6 to 8

I have fond memories of enjoying this soup on layovers in Italy. A glass of wine and plenty of crusty Italian bread—what more could you ask for!

2 tbsp	olive oil	25 ml
3 oz	pancetta or bacon, chopped (optional)	90 g
3	small onions, sliced into rings	3
4	cloves garlic, minced	4
2	stalks celery, sliced	2
2	carrots, scraped and sliced	2
2 cups	chopped Savoy cabbage or kale	500 ml
¼ tsp	hot pepper flakes or to taste	1 ml
3 cups	low-sodium beef or vegetable stock	750 ml
3 cups	water	750 ml
1	can (28 oz/796 ml) plum tomatoes, chopped	1
2 tbsp	chopped fresh basil or 2 tsp/10 ml dried basil	25 ml
½ cup	red wine	125 ml
2 cups	white kidney beans, cooked or canned (drained and rinsed)	500 ml
½ cup	macaroni or other small-shaped pasta sea salt and freshly ground pepper to taste	125 ml
Garnish:	freshly grated or shaved Parmesan cheese (optional)	

1. In a large saucepan, heat 1 tbsp/15 ml of oil over medium heat. Add pancetta and cook for 5 minutes or until crisp. (If using bacon, omit the oil.) Drain on paper towel and set aside.
2. In saucepan, heat remaining oil over medium heat. Add onions, garlic and celery; sauté for 6 minutes.
3. Add carrots, cabbage, hot pepper flakes, stock, water, tomatoes with juice, basil, red wine and beans; bring to a boil. Reduce heat, cover and simmer for 15 minutes.
4. Bring to a gentle boil and add pancetta and pasta; simmer for 10 minutes or until pasta is tender but firm, stirring occasionally. Season with salt and pepper and serve with Parmesan cheese, if desired.

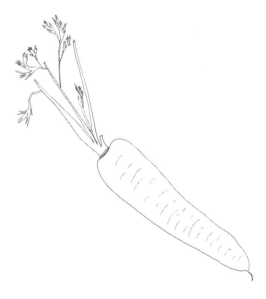

Scotch Broth with Meatballs

Serves 6 to 8

This is a twist on an old favourite. Moist and tender meatballs accompanied by lots of vegetables and a tasty broth make this soup a winning combination.

Meatballs

	oil or non-stick cooking spray	
1 lb	lean ground lamb	500 g
½ cup	dry bread crumbs	125 ml
2	cloves garlic, minced	2
2 tbsp	finely chopped fresh Italian parsley	25 ml
1	egg, slightly beaten	1
	sea salt and freshly ground pepper to taste	

Preheat oven to 350°F/180°C.

1. Rub a small amount of oil or use non-stick cooking spray on a baking sheet.
2. In a bowl, combine all ingredients. Shape meat mixture into 1-inch/ 2.5-cm balls. Place meatballs on baking sheet and bake for 15 minutes. Drain on paper towel and set aside.

     ↵ Tip: Dampen hands or rub them with a little oil before rolling meatballs to prevent meat from sticking.

Microwave directions:
Place half of the meatballs on a microwave dish and cover with waxed paper. Cook on medium heat for 4 to 6 minutes or until no longer pink. Remove from plate, repeat with remaining meatballs and drain on paper towels, set aside.

For the Love of Soup

Soup

1 tbsp	olive or safflower oil	15 ml
1	onion, chopped	1
3	cloves garlic, minced	3
2	stalks celery, finely chopped	2
$\frac{1}{3}$ cup	barley	80 ml
4 cups	low-sodium beef or vegetable stock	1 L
4 cups	water	1 L
1	bay leaf	1
1 tsp	chopped fresh thyme	5 ml
	or $\frac{1}{2}$ tsp/2 ml dried thyme	
2	carrots, scraped and diced	2
2 cups	peeled, diced turnip or rutabaga	500 ml
1	large potato, peeled and diced	1
	sea salt and freshly ground pepper to taste	

1. In a large saucepan, heat oil over medium heat. Add onion, garlic and celery; sauté for 4 minutes. Stir in barley and cook for 2 minutes longer.
2. Add stock, water, bay leaf, thyme, carrots, turnip, potato and meatballs; bring to a boil. Reduce heat, cover and simmer for 30 to 40 minutes or until barley is tender, stirring occasionally. Remove bay leaf and season with salt and pepper.

> ↪Tip: A thin layer of fat from the meatballs will surface on your soup. Skim fat before serving. By making your soup ahead of time and refrigerating, you can easily remove hardened fat before reheating.

Spicy Black Bean Chili Soup

Serves 6 to 8

This South American-inspired soup is wholesome and delicious. It is a great make-ahead soup for casual entertaining.

4	strips bacon, chopped (optional)	4
1 tbsp	olive or safflower oil	15 ml
1	large onion, finely chopped	1
1	sweet red pepper, finely chopped	1
1	celery stalk, finely chopped	1
2	cloves garlic, minced	2
1 tbsp	chopped fresh oregano	15 ml
	or 1 tsp/5 ml dried oregano	
¼ tsp	hot chili flakes or to taste	1 ml
1 tsp	cumin powder	5 ml
1	large carrot, scraped and finely chopped	1
1	large potato, peeled and diced	1
3 cups	low-sodium chicken or vegetable stock	750 ml
2 cups	water	500 ml
1	can (19 oz/540 ml) tomatoes, chopped	1
2	cans (each 19 oz/540 ml) black beans, drained and rinsed	2
¼ cup	chopped fresh cilantro	50 ml

1. In a large saucepan, cook bacon over medium heat until crisp. Drain and set aside.
2. In saucepan, heat oil over medium heat. Add onion, red pepper, celery and garlic; sauté for 4 minutes. Stir in oregano, chili flakes and cumin powder; cook for 2 minutes longer.
3. Add carrot, potato, stock and water, tomatoes with juice, beans and bacon; bring to a boil. Reduce heat, cover and simmer for 20 minutes, stirring occasionally. Gently stir in fresh cilantro.

For the Love of Soup

Vegetable Beef Curry Soup

Serves 4 to 6

This soup was inspired by my Mom's favourite ground beef recipe. I enjoyed her dish so much when I was growing up that I decided to convert it to a soup.

2 tbsp	olive or safflower oil	25 ml
12 oz	lean ground beef	375 ml
1	onion, chopped	1
2	cloves garlic, minced	2
2	carrots, scraped and diced	2
2 cups	peeled, diced turnip or rutabaga	500 ml
2 tsp	mild curry paste	10 ml
¼ tsp	hot pepper flakes or to taste	1 ml
2 cups	low-sodium beef stock	500 ml
1 cup	water	250 ml
1 cup	fresh or canned tomatoes, diced	250 ml
	sea salt and freshly ground pepper to taste	

1. In a large saucepan, heat 1 tbsp/15 ml of oil over medium heat. Add beef and cook, breaking up meat with a wooden spoon, for about 4 minutes or until meat is no longer pink. Drain off fat and transfer meat to a plate.
2. Heat remaining oil in saucepan and add onion, garlic, carrots and turnip; sauté vegetables for 4 minutes. Return meat to saucepan; add curry and hot pepper flakes and sauté for 2 minutes longer.
3. Add stock, water and tomatoes; bring to a boil. Reduce heat; cover and simmer for 20 minutes or until vegetables are tender, stirring occasionally. Season with salt and pepper

↭ Tip: For a thinner consistency, add extra stock or water.

There is no love sincerer
than the love of food.

George Bernard Shaw

Seafood Soups

Capture the Healthy Treasures from the Sea

Let the beauty we love be what we do.

Remi

Asian-Style Fish Soup

Serves 6

Marinating the fish gives this soup a wonderful flavour and the rice adds a thick, creamy texture.

1 lb	firm white fish fillets, such as cod, haddock, or halibut, cut into bite-sized pieces	500 g
2 tbsp	low-sodium soy sauce	25 ml
1 tsp	sesame oil	5 ml
2 tbsp	safflower oil	25 ml
1	onion, chopped	1
2	cloves garlic, minced	2
2	stalks celery, sliced diagonally	2
2	carrots, scraped and sliced diagonally	2
4	green onions, chopped	4
¼ cup	long-grain rice	50 ml
4 cups	low-sodium chicken or vegetable stock	1 L
2 cups	water	500 ml
1 tbsp	rice vinegar or fresh lemon juice	15 ml
	hot pepper sauce to taste	

1. Place fish pieces into a bowl. Combine soy sauce and sesame oil and add to fish; cover and marinate in the refrigerator.
2. Meanwhile, in a large saucepan, heat safflower oil over medium heat. Add onion, garlic and celery; sauté for 4 minutes.
3. Stir in carrots, green onions, rice, stock, water, rice vinegar or lemon juice and hot pepper sauce; bring to a boil. Reduce heat, cover and simmer for 15 minutes or until rice is tender.
4. Gently stir in fish with marinade and simmer for 4 minutes or until fish is cooked.

↩ Tip: Remember to be careful when cooking fish because it toughens with over-cooking or when reheating.

Clam & Corn Chowder

Serves 4

*I remember when my mother first made clam chowder.
I was not fond of clams but quickly developed a taste
for them, once I tried her soup. My sister gave me her
recipe, adding corn and red pepper.*

1 tbsp	unsalted butter	15 ml
1	onion, chopped	1
2	stalks celery, diced	2
1	sweet red pepper, diced	1
2	medium potatoes, peeled and diced	2
1 cup	fresh or frozen kernel corn	250 ml
1 tbsp	chopped fresh thyme	15 ml
	or 1 tsp/5 ml dried thyme	
1	bay leaf	1
1 cup	low-sodium chicken or vegetable stock	250 ml
1 cup	water	250 ml
1 cup	low-fat milk	250 ml
1 tbsp	cornstarch	15 ml
1	can (10 oz/284 ml) baby clams,	1
	drained, liquid reserved	
	sea salt and freshly ground pepper to taste	
Garnish:	chopped fresh parsley or cilantro	

1. In a large saucepan, melt butter over medium heat. Add onion, celery and red pepper; sauté for 4 minutes.
2. Stir in potatoes, corn, thyme, bay leaf, stock, water and drained liquid from the clams; bring to a boil. Reduce heat; cover and simmer for 15 minutes or until potatoes are tender, stirring occasionally.
3. Combine milk and cornstarch in a jar with a tight fitting lid and shake until well blended and add to saucepan along with clams; simmer, stirring frequently until the soup starts to thicken slightly, about 5 minutes. Season with salt and pepper and serve garnished with parsley or cilantro.

Newfoundland Seafood Chowder

Serves 6 to 8

For the seafood lover, this tantalizing medley of seafood and vegetables is super-satisfying.

1 tbsp	unsalted butter	15 ml
1	leek, white and light part only, finely chopped	1
1	onion, finely chopped	1
1	stalk celery, diced	1
1	small sweet red pepper, diced	1
3	medium potatoes, peeled and diced	3
2 cups	low-sodium chicken or vegetable stock	500 ml
1 cup	water	250 ml
1 tbsp	chopped fresh thyme or 1 tsp/5 ml dried thyme	15 ml
1	bay leaf	1
1 lb	bag frozen mixed seafood (scallops, small peeled shrimp, clams, squid, mussels), thawed	500 g
2 cups	low-fat milk	500 ml
2 tbsp	cornstarch	25 ml
	sea salt and freshly ground pepper to taste	
Garnish:	chopped fresh Italian parsley	

1. In a large saucepan, melt butter over medium heat. Add leek, onion, celery and red pepper; sauté for 4 minutes. Stir in potatoes, stock, water, thyme and bay leaf; bring to a boil. Reduce heat, cover and simmer for 15 minutes or until potatoes are tender, stirring occasionally. Add the mixed seafood and simmer for 3 minutes.
2. Combine milk and cornstarch in a jar with a tight fitting lid and shake until well blended and add to saucepan. Simmer until the soup starts to thicken slightly, about 5 minutes, stirring frequently. Season with salt and pepper and serve garnished with parsley.

Curried Tuna Chowder

Serves 4 to 6

Hearty, nutritious and easy to prepare, this chowder is a great meal-in-a-bowl.

1 tbsp	safflower oil	15 ml
1	onion, chopped	1
2	cloves garlic, minced	2
2	stalks celery, diced	2
1	carrot, scraped and diced	1
2 tsp	mild curry paste	10 ml
¼ cup	short-grain rice	50 ml
3 cups	water	750 ml
1	can (19 oz/540 ml) tomatoes, chopped	1
1 cup	low-fat milk	250 ml
1 tbsp	cornstarch	15 ml
1	can (6½ oz/170 g) albacore tuna, packed in water (do not drain)	1
	sea salt and freshly ground pepper to taste	

1. In a large saucepan, heat oil over medium heat. Add onion, garlic and celery; sauté for 4 minutes. Stir in carrot, curry and rice; cook for 2 minutes longer.
2. Add water and tomatoes with juice; bring to a boil. Reduce heat, cover and simmer for 15 minutes or until rice is tender.
3. Combine milk and cornstarch in a jar with a tight fitting lid and shake until well blended and add to saucepan. Stir in tuna and simmer until the soup starts to thicken slightly, about 5 minutes, stirring frequently. Season with salt and pepper.

Fish Soup
with Tomato & Oregano

Serves 6 to 8

Growing up in Grand Falls, New Brunswick, we always had fish on Fridays, most often served with locally grown potatoes. This soup pays homage to those dinners.

1 tbsp	olive or safflower oil	15 ml
1	onion, chopped	1
3	cloves garlic, minced	3
1	small sweet green pepper, chopped	1
2	stalks celery, sliced	2
2	carrots, scraped and sliced	2
2	potatoes, peeled and cubed	2
2 cups	low-sodium chicken or vegetable stock	500 ml
1 cup	water	250 ml
½ cup	dry white wine	125 ml
1	can (19 oz/540 ml) tomatoes, chopped	1
1 tbsp	chopped fresh oregano or 1 tsp/5 ml dried oregano	15 ml
1 tbsp	Worcestershire sauce	15 ml
2 tbsp	chopped fresh parsley	25 ml
1 lb	fish fillet, such as haddock or cod, cut into bite-sized pieces	500 g
2 tbsp	fresh lemon juice	25 ml
	sea salt and freshly ground pepper to taste	

1. In a large saucepan, heat oil over medium heat. Add onion, garlic, green pepper and celery; sauté for 4 minutes.
2. Add carrots, potatoes, stock, water, white wine, tomatoes with juice, oregano, Worcestershire and parsley; bring to a boil. Reduce heat, cover and simmer for 15 minutes.
3. Gently stir in fish and simmer for 4 minutes or until fish is cooked. Add lemon juice and season with salt and pepper.

Greek-Style
Shrimp & Orzo Soup with Feta

Serves 4 to 6

Orzo, a rice-shaped pasta, is a staple of many Mediterranean soups. My hairdresser Sal once told me about a tomato, shrimp and feta dish he enjoyed on a holiday. The dish sounded so good that I added some orzo and came up with this recipe for a fabulous Greek-inspired soup.

1 tbsp	olive oil	15 ml
1	large onion, chopped	1
3	cloves garlic, minced	3
1	sweet red or green pepper, chopped	1
2 cups	low-sodium fish, chicken or vegetable stock	500 ml
1 tbsp	chopped fresh oregano or 1 tsp/5 ml dried oregano	15 ml
2 cups	water	500 ml
1	can (19 oz/540 ml) tomatoes, chopped	1
½ cup	orzo	125 ml
1 lb	medium raw shrimp, shelled and deveined	500 g
2 tbsp	fresh lemon juice	25 ml
	sea salt and freshly ground pepper to taste	
¾ cup	crumbled low-fat feta cheese	175 ml
Garnish:	chopped fresh Italian parsley	

1. In a large saucepan, heat oil over medium heat. Add onion, garlic and red or green pepper; sauté for 4 minutes. Add stock, oregano, water, and tomatoes with juice; bring to a boil. Add orzo and cook for 10 minutes or until tender but firm.
2. Stir in shrimp and lemon juice, simmer for 3 minutes or until shrimp are opaque in colour. Season with salt and pepper and serve with crumbled feta cheese and garnish with parsley.

Tip: Cooking shrimp takes mere minutes. Overcooking will cause them to become tough.

Mediterranean Seafood Soup with Fresh Herbs

Serves 4 to 6

Fresh herbs add a delightful flavour to this elegant soup.
It's perfect as a starter for a dinner party.

1 tbsp	olive or safflower oil	15 ml
6	cloves garlic, minced	6
1	medium red onion, cut in half and thinly sliced	1
2	stalks celery, cut in julienne strips (size of matchsticks)	2
2	carrots, scraped and cut in julienne strips	2
2 cups	low-sodium fish or chicken stock	500 ml
2 cups	water	500 ml
¾ cup	dry white wine	175 ml
3	large plum tomatoes, diced	3
1 tbsp	chopped fresh sage	15 ml
2 tsp	chopped fresh basil	10 ml
1 tsp	chopped fresh thyme	5 ml
1	juice of 1 lemon	1
1 lb	fresh mussels or clams	500 g
8 oz	medium raw shrimp, peeled and deveined	250 g
12 oz	fresh or frozen boneless fish fillets, such as haddock, cod or sole, cut in chunks	375 g
	sea salt and freshly ground pepper to taste	

1. In a large saucepan, heat oil over medium heat. Add garlic, onion, celery and carrots; sauté for 4 minutes. Add stock, water, wine, tomatoes, sage, basil, thyme and lemon juice; bring to a boil. Reduce heat, cover and simmer for 10 minutes.
2. Add mussels or clams, shrimp and chunks of fish; continue to simmer for 6 minutes or until mussels have opened, and season with salt and pepper.

> ↭ Tip: To store uncooked mussels, place them in an open container with a damp towel over top and refrigerate. Rinse and scrub mussels just before cooking. Discard any mussels with cracked shells or any that do not close when tapped. Once cooked, discard any mussels that are closed.

Hearty Fish Soup
with Fennel

Serves 6

The subtle flavour of the fennel complements the fish in this nutritious soup.

1 tbsp	olive or safflower oil	15 ml
1	large onion, chopped	1
2	cloves garlic, minced	2
1	sweet green pepper, chopped	1
1	medium fennel bulb, cubed, feathery green ends discarded	1
2 cups	low-sodium chicken or vegetable stock	500 ml
2 cup	water	500 ml
2	medium potatoes, peeled and cubed	2
1 tbsp	chopped fresh basil or 1 tsp/5 ml dried basil	15 ml
½ tsp	fennel seeds	2 ml
	dash hot pepper sauce	
1	can (28 oz/796 ml) tomatoes, chopped	1
2 tbsp	fresh lemon juice	25 ml
1½ lbs	fish fillets such as haddock or cod, cut in bite-size pieces	750 g
	sea salt and freshly ground pepper to taste	

1. In a large saucepan, heat oil over medium heat. Add onion, garlic, green pepper and fennel; sauté for 6 minutes.
2. Add stock, water, potatoes, basil, fennel seeds, hot pepper sauce, tomatoes with juice and lemon juice; bring to boil. Reduce heat, cover and simmer for 15 minutes or until fennel is tender. Gently add fish pieces and simmer for 5 minutes or until fish is cooked. Season with salt and pepper.

Mussels in Tomato Wine Broth

Serves 4 to 6

Mussels yield a delicious liquid when cooked. Serve this soup with plenty of crusty bread for dunking.

1 tbsp	olive or safflower oil	15 ml
1	onion, finely chopped	1
4	cloves garlic, minced	4
1	stalk celery, finely chopped	1
2 cups	low-sodium chicken or fish stock	500 ml
1 cup	water	250 ml
1 cup	white wine	250 ml
1	can (28 oz/796 ml) diced tomatoes, or 2 lbs/1 kg fresh tomatoes	1
2 tbsp	chopped fresh thyme or 1 tsp/5 ml dried thyme	25 ml 1 tsp
1 tsp	Worcestershire sauce	5 ml
2 tbsp	fresh lemon juice	25 ml
	dash hot pepper sauce or to taste	
2 lbs	fresh mussels (see page 145)	1 kg
Garnish:	chopped fresh parsley or chives	

1. In a large saucepan, heat oil over medium heat. Add onions, garlic and celery; sauté for 4 minutes. Add stock, water, wine, tomatoes with juice, thyme, Worcestershire sauce, lemon juice, hot pepper sauce and bring to a boil. Reduce heat, cover and simmer for 10 minutes.
2. Add mussels, cover and simmer for 8 minutes or until mussels are cooked, stirring occasionally. Serve garnished with fresh parsley or chives.

Salmon & Spring Vegetable Chowder with Dijon

Serves 4 to 6

Celebrate spring with this fabulously fresh chowder. The combination of salmon, spring vegetables and Dijon creates an unusual and inspired soup.

1 tbsp	unsalted butter	15 ml
1	onion, chopped	1
2	stalks celery, sliced	2
3 cups	low-sodium chicken or vegetable stock	750 ml
6 to 8	small red new potatoes, scrubbed and quartered	6 to 8
1 cup	baby carrots, scrubbed and halved	250 ml
12	asparagus spears, trimmed and cut diagonally in thirds	12
1 cup	low-fat milk	250 ml
2 tbsp	cornstarch	25 ml
1 lb	salmon fillet, skin removed, cut in bite-sized chunks	500 g
1 tbsp	Dijon mustard	15 ml
1 tsp	lemon zest	5 ml
1 tbsp	finely chopped fresh dill or 1 tsp/5 ml dried dill	15 ml
	sea salt and freshly ground pepper to taste	
Garnish:	chopped fresh dill or parsley	

For the Love of Soup

1. In a large saucepan, melt butter over medium heat. Add onion and celery; sauté for 4 minutes. Add stock, potatoes, carrots and asparagus; bring to a boil. Reduce heat, cover and simmer for 15 minutes.
2. Combine milk and cornstarch in a jar with a tight fitting lid and shake until well blended and stir into the saucepan. Add salmon, Dijon, lemon zest and dill, simmer for 5 minutes until the soup starts to thicken slightly, stirring occasionally. Season with salt and pepper and serve garnished with fresh dill or parsley.

↬ Tip: The freshest fish is available on Fridays. That's when the demand is greatest.

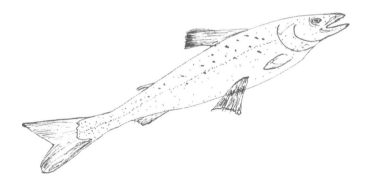

Thai Shrimp & Noodle Soup

Serves 6 to 8

My friend Gale gets the credit for introducing me to the exotic flavours of Thai cooking. This soup is a recent addition to my recipe collection and was an instant hit at a recent dinner party.

2 oz	rice stick noodles (about 1 cup/250 ml)	60 g
1 tbsp	safflower oil	15 ml
1	small onion, coarsely chopped	1
2	cloves garlic, slightly crushed	2
2	stalks lemon grass, trimmed and coarsely chopped	2
1	1-inch/2.5-cm piece of gingerroot, sliced	1
1	Thai or serrano chili pepper, sliced lengthwise and seeded	1
4 cups	low-sodium fish or chicken stock	1 L
4 cups	water	1 L
4	kaffir lime leaves	4
1 tbsp	fish sauce	15 ml
1 tbsp	low-sodium soy sauce	15 ml
12 oz	medium raw shrimp, peeled and deveined (shells reserved)	375 g
1	large carrot, cut in fine julienne (size of matchsticks)	1
Garnish:	green onions, thinly sliced diagonally fresh cilantro leaves	

1. Place rice noodles in a medium bowl; pour boiling water over them to cover and let soak until noodles are tender, about 10 minutes. Drain and set aside.

2. In a large saucepan, heat oil over medium heat. Add onion, garlic, lemon grass, gingerroot, chili pepper and shrimp shells; sauté for 4 minutes. Add stock, water, lime leaves, fish sauce and soy sauce; bring to a boil. Reduce heat and simmer for 15 minutes. Remove from heat, strain liquid through a sieve and discard solids.

3. Pour liquid into saucepan and bring to a boil; add shrimp, carrots and noodles; simmer for 3 to 4 minutes or until shrimp are pink in colour. Serve garnished with green onions and cilantro leaves.

> Tip: Lemon grass, fish sauce and kaffir lime leaves can be found in Asian markets and well-stocked supermarkets.

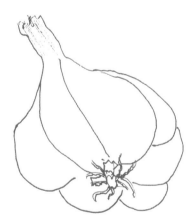

Cajun-Style Fish Soup

Serves 4 to 6

In my 30 years as a flight attendant, I never made it to New Orleans. This savoury soup is a Mardi Gras for the taste buds!

1 tbsp	olive or safflower oil	15 ml
1	large onion, chopped	1
2	cloves garlic, minced	2
1	sweet green pepper, chopped	1
1	carrot, scraped and sliced	1
⅓ cup	long-grain rice	80 ml
2 tsp	chili powder	10 ml
¼ tsp	red pepper flakes	1 ml
1 tbsp	chopped fresh oregano	15 ml
	or 1 tsp/5 ml dried oregano	
1	bay leaf	1
2 cups	low-sodium chicken or fish stock	500 ml
2 cups	water	500 ml
1	can (28 oz/796 ml) diced stewed tomatoes	1
1 lb	fresh red snapper fillets cut in bite-sized chunks	500 g
	sea salt and freshly ground pepper to taste	

1. In a large saucepan, heat oil over medium heat. Add onion, garlic, green pepper and carrot; sauté for 4 minutes. Stir in rice and cook for 1 minute longer.

2. Add chili powder, red pepper flakes, oregano, bay leaf, stock, water and tomatoes with juice; bring to a boil. Reduce heat, cover and simmer for 15 minutes or until rice is cooked. Gently stir in fish and simmer for 4 minutes or until fish is cooked. Season with salt and pepper.

↩ Tip: You can substitute any fish or shellfish for the red snapper.

For the Love of Soup

Chilled Soups

Capture that Cooler-than-Cool Feeling

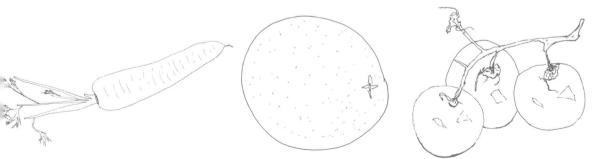

Love is, above all, the gift of oneself.

Jean Anduilh

Mango Orange Soup

This tasty summer sensation can be enjoyed any time of day.

2	ripe mangoes, peeled, pitted and diced	2
2 cups	fresh orange juice	500 ml
1 cup	white grape juice	250 ml
½ tsp	vanilla	2 ml
1 cup	low-fat yogurt	250 ml
1 cup	water	250 ml
Garnish:	orange zest	

1. Combine mangoes, orange juice, grape juice, vanilla, yogurt and water in blender and blend until smooth.
2. Transfer to a bowl, cover and refrigerate for at least 1 hour before serving. Serve garnished with orange zest.

Bean Gazpacho

Serves 4 to 6

I first made this tasty, healthy soup on a hot summer day when Tim's cousin Mary and her family were visiting at the cottage. Mary, who painted the cover image for this book, helped me refine this recipe and gave the soup its name.

2	cans (each 19 oz/540 ml) mixed beans, drained and rinsed	2
1	can (28 oz/796 ml) tomatoes	1
1 cup	low-sodium vegetable or chicken stock	250 ml
2	green onions, finely sliced	2
¼ cup	chopped fresh cilantro or Italian parsley	50 ml
1 tsp	chili powder	5 ml
1 tsp	cumin powder	5 ml
2	juice of 2 limes	2
	dash hot pepper sauce	
2 or 3	ripe tomatoes, diced	2 or 3
1	sweet green pepper, diced	1
½ cup	sliced black olives (optional)	125 ml

1. Combine beans and canned tomatoes with juice in a large bowl. Purée using an immersion blender or transfer in 2 batches to a blender or food processor and blend, adding half of stock to each batch. (Add extra if a thinner consistency is desired.) Return to large bowl.

2. Stir in green onions, cilantro or parsley, chili powder, cumin, lime juice and hot pepper sauce; refrigerate until chilled and ready to serve. Ladle soup into bowls. Serve passing diced tomatoes, diced green pepper and sliced black olives, if desired, separately.

For the Love of Soup

Chilled Beet Soup

This brilliantly coloured soup makes a great summer starter. Don't spill this on your new white shirt!

2 lbs	small young beets	1 kg
	water for boiling beets	
	(save 3 cups/750 ml for soup)	
1 tbsp	unsalted butter	15 ml
2	medium leeks, white and light parts only, chopped	2
2	cloves garlic, minced	2
1	large carrot, scraped and chopped	1
2 cups	low-sodium chicken or vegetable stock	500 ml
1 tbsp	fresh lemon juice	15 ml
Garnish:	low-fat sour cream (optional)	
	snipped fresh chives or green onions	

1. Wash beets and trim, leaving a little of the ends attached. In a large saucepan, cover beets with water and bring to a boil. Reduce heat, cover and simmer for 30 minutes or until beets are tender. Drain, reserving 3 cups/750 ml of cooking liquid. Under cold running water, rub off the peel (the peel will come off easily). Remove the ends, coarsely chop beets and set aside.
2. In a large saucepan, melt butter over medium heat. Add leeks, garlic and carrot; sauté for 4 minutes. Add stock, reserved cooking liquid, beets and lemon juice; bring to a boil. Reduce heat, cover and simmer for 15 minutes. Remove from heat and cool slightly.
3. Purée soup in saucepan using an immersion blender or transfer in batches to a blender or food processor and blend until smooth. Transfer soup into a large bowl, cover and refrigerate until chilled. Serve garnished with sour cream, if desired, and snipped chives or green onions.

Carrot Vichyssoise

Serves 4 to 6

My husband Tim can't get enough of this creamy, refreshing soup.

1 tbsp	olive or safflower oil	15 ml
2	large leeks, white and light parts only, chopped	2
2	cloves garlic, chopped	2
3 cups	scraped and chopped carrots	750 ml
1	large baking potato, peeled and chopped	1
2 cups	low-sodium chicken or vegetable stock	500 ml
2 cups	water	500 ml
1 cup	low-fat buttermilk	250 ml
	sea salt and freshly ground pepper to taste	
Garnish:	chopped fresh mint or snipped chives	

1. In a large saucepan, heat oil over medium heat. Add leeks and garlic; sauté for 6 minutes. Add carrots, potato, stock and water; bring to a boil. Reduce heat, cover and simmer for 20 minutes, stirring occasionally. Remove from heat and cool slightly.

2. Purée soup in saucepan using an immersion blender or transfer in batches to a blender or food processor and blend until smooth. Place soup into a large bowl, cover and refrigerate until chilled. Just before serving add buttermilk and season with salt and pepper. Serve garnished with mint or chives.

Chilled Cucumber-Yogurt Soup

Serves 4 to 6

This soup is cooler-than-cool on a hot summer day.
Quick to make for a summer lunch on the dock.

2	large cucumbers, peeled	2
	sea salt for salting cucumbers	
2	cloves garlic, minced	2
¼ cup	chopped fresh dill	50 ml
¼ cup	chopped fresh Italian parsley	50 ml
1	juice of 1 lemon or to taste	1
	freshly ground pepper to taste	
1 tsp	sugar	5 ml
1 cup	chilled low-sodium vegetable stock	250 ml
2 cups	low-fat yogurt	500 ml
1 cup	skim or low-fat milk	250 ml
Garnish:	snipped fresh chives	

1. Cut cucumbers in half lengthwise, scoop out the seeds and discard. Grate the cucumbers and place them in a large strainer. Place the strainer over the bowl in which you will serve the soup. Salt the cucumbers lightly and let stand for 20 minutes (the juice from the cucumbers will drain into the bowl and the cucumbers will become pleasantly crisp).
2. Transfer grated cucumbers to the bowl; add garlic, dill, parsley, lemon juice, pepper, sugar, stock, yogurt and milk. Add extra stock or milk if a thinner consistency is desired. Cover and refrigerate for 1 hour before serving. Serve garnished with chives.

Chilled Tarragon-Tomato Bisque

Serves 4 to 6

A cool blend of herbs and vegetables. Rice is the secret "creamy" ingredient.

1 tbsp	olive oil	15 ml
1	large sweet white onion, chopped	1
4	large shallots, chopped	4
3 lbs	fresh ripe tomatoes (about 4 large)	1.5 kg
¼ cup	short-grain white rice	50 ml
1 cup	low-sodium chicken or vegetable stock	250 ml
2 cups	water	500 ml
1 tsp	balsamic vinegar	5 ml
1 tsp	sugar	5 ml
1 tbsp	fresh lemon juice	15 ml
1 tbsp	finely chopped fresh tarragon	15 ml
	sea salt and freshly ground pepper to taste	
Garnish:	chopped fresh tarragon	

1. In a large saucepan, heat oil over medium heat. Add onion and shallots; sauté for 4 minutes. Stir in tomatoes, rice, stock and water, balsamic vinegar, sugar, lemon juice and tarragon; bring to a boil. Reduce heat, cover and simmer for 20 minutes or until rice is tender. Remove from heat and cool slightly.

2. Purée soup in saucepan using an immersion blender or transfer in batches to a blender or food processor and blend until smooth. Season with salt and pepper; refrigerate covered for 2 hours or until chilled. Serve garnished with a sprinkling of tarragon.

↜ Tip: You can also enjoy this soup heated on a cool day.

Chilled Petit Pois Soup with Mint

Serves 6 to 8

I never knew peas could taste so good. A hint of mint gives this soup a wonderful fresh taste.

1 tbsp	unsalted butter	15 ml
2	leeks, white and light parts only, finely chopped	2
4	green onions, finely chopped	4
2 cups	low-sodium chicken or vegetable stock	500 ml
2 cups	water	500 ml
3 cups	fresh or frozen tiny peas	750 ml
1	medium head romaine or iceberg lettuce, chopped	1
2 tbsp	finely chopped fresh mint	25 ml
1 tsp	sugar	5 ml
Garnish:	low-fat yogurt or sour cream (optional) fresh mint sprigs	

1. In a large saucepan, melt butter over medium heat. Add leeks and green onions; sauté for 4 minutes. Add stock, water and peas; bring to a boil. Reduce heat, cover and simmer for 15 minutes, stirring occasionally.

2. Add lettuce, mint and sugar; simmer for 5 minutes longer. Remove from heat and cool slightly.

3. Purée soup in saucepan using an immersion blender or transfer in batches to a blender or food processor and blend until smooth. Place soup into a large bowl; cover and refrigerate until chilled. Serve garnished with a dollop of yogurt or sour cream, if desired, and mint sprigs.

Chilled Strawberry Soup

Glass bowls are pretty for serving this delicious soup when you're entertaining guests.

4 cups	fresh strawberries	1 L
1 cup	cranberry juice	250 ml
1 cup	water	250 ml
1 cup	low-fat yogurt	250 ml
1 tbsp	sugar	15 ml
1 tbsp	finely chopped fresh mint	15 ml
1	juice of 1 lemon	1
Garnish:	reserved sliced strawberries	

1. Slice 6 strawberries for garnish and set aside.
2. In a large bowl, combine remaining strawberries, cranberry juice, water, yogurt, sugar, mint and lemon juice.
3. Purée the mixture in the bowl using an immersion blender or transfer in batches to a blender or food processor and blend until smooth. Transfer soup to a bowl, cover and refrigerate at least 1 hour before serving. Serve garnished with strawberry slices.

Cream of Greens Soup

Serves 4 to 6

When my friend Marilyn came to visit at the cottage, we shared a lot of memories over a bowl of this healthy and delicious soup.

1 tbsp	unsalted butter	15 ml
8	green onions, chopped	8
2 cups	low-sodium chicken or vegetable stock	500 ml
2 cups	water	500 ml
1	medium baking potato, peeled and diced	1
2 cups	peeled, chopped English cucumber	500 ml
2 cups	chopped spinach	500 ml
1 tbsp	chopped fresh basil	15 ml
	or 1 tsp/5 ml dried basil	
1 tbsp	chopped fresh thyme	15 ml
	or 1 tsp/5 ml dried thyme	
2 tbsp	lemon juice	25 ml
	sea salt and freshly ground pepper to taste	
Garnish:	low-fat sour cream or yogurt (optional)	
	snipped fresh chives or green onion	

1. In a large saucepan, melt butter over medium heat. Add green onions and sauté for 2 minutes.
2. Add stock, water, potato, cucumber, spinach, basil, thyme and lemon juice; bring to a boil. Reduce heat, cover and simmer for 15 minutes or until the vegetables are tender. Remove from heat and cool slightly.
3. Purée soup in saucepan using an immersion blender or transfer in batches to a blender or food processor and blend until smooth. Season with salt and pepper. Place soup into a bowl, cover and refrigerate until chilled. Serve garnished with sour cream or yogurt, if desired, and snipped chives or green onions.

Cool Black Bean, Corn & Salsa Soup

Serves 4 to 6

A chunky mix of colourful vegetables highlighted with fresh cilantro, this soup is a feast for the eyes as well as the palate.

2	large ripe tomatoes, coarsely chopped	2
1 cup	canned black beans, drained and rinsed	250 ml
1 cup	cooked corn kernels	250 ml
2	large ripe tomatoes, finely chopped	2
1	fresh jalapeno pepper, seeded and finely chopped	1
3	green onions, finely chopped	3
¼ cup	chopped fresh cilantro	50 ml
1	clove garlic, minced	1
1 tsp	sugar	5 ml
1	juice of 1 lime	1
	sea salt and freshly ground pepper to taste	
Garnish:	fat-free tortilla chips (optional)	

1. Purée 2 chopped tomatoes in a food processor or blender until smooth and pour into a large bowl.
2. Stir in black beans, corn, finely chopped tomatoes, jalapeno pepper, green onions, cilantro, garlic, sugar and lime juice. Season with salt and pepper and serve immediately or chill until needed. Garnish each serving with 2 tortilla chips.

For the Love of Soup

Gazpacho My Way

Serves 4 to 6

There is nothing more intimidating than making gazpacho for a Spaniard. My Spanish friend Conchita told me that gazpacho "my way" was the only way to enjoy this classic chilled soup.

6	medium ripe tomatoes, coarsely chopped	6
1	cucumber, peeled, seeded and chopped	1
2	stalks celery, chopped	2
2	sweet red peppers, chopped	2
1	sweet green pepper, chopped	1
1	small red onion, chopped	1
2	cloves garlic, minced	2
2 tbsp	tomato paste	25 ml
¼ cup	olive oil	50 ml
1 tbsp	balsamic or red wine vinegar	15 ml
1	juice of 1 lime, or to taste	1
	dash hot pepper sauce, or to taste	
1 cup	tomato juice (optional)	250 ml
	sea salt and freshly ground pepper to taste	
Garnish:	chopped fresh cilantro or Italian parsley	

1. Place tomatoes, cucumber, celery, red pepper, green pepper, onion, garlic and tomato paste in a large bowl.
2. Transfer in batches to a blender or food processor. Process the vegetables until they are minced, still retaining texture, adding some of the oil to each batch. Transfer to a large bowl.
3. Add vinegar, lime juice and hot pepper sauce. Thin with tomato juice, if desired, and season with salt and pepper. Cover and refrigerate until needed. Serve garnished with cilantro or parsley.

Index

R

S

T

Successful Cooking

Happy and successful cooking doesn't rely only on know-how; it comes from the heart, makes great demands on the palate and needs enthusiasm and a deep love of food to bring it to life.

(Unknown)